BREAKFASTS

ALMOND FRITTATA

Serving: 6

Ingredients:

- ½ cup tomatoes, cubed
- 1 cup almond milk
- ½ cup beef, chopped
- 2 spring onions, chopped
- 12 eggs, whisked
- A pinch of salt and black pepper
- A drizzle of olive oil

Directions:

- In a bowl, mix the all the ingredients except the oil and whisk well.
- Grease the slow cooker with the oil then pour the frittata mix in the bowl, spread, cover and cook on low for 3 hours.
- Divide between plates and serve for breakfast.

Nutrition:

- Calories - 295
- Fat - 22,4
- Carbs - 3,9
- Protein - 20,8

BUTTERNUT SQUASH BREAKFAST MIX

Serving: 4

Ingredients:

- 2 apples, peeled, cored and cubed
- ½ cup walnuts, soaked for 12 hours and drained
- ½ cup almonds
- 1 butternut squash, peeled and cubed
- 1 teaspoon cinnamon powder
- ½ teaspoon nutmeg, ground
- 1 tablespoon coconut sugar
- 1 cup coconut milk

Directions:

- In your slow cooker, mix walnuts with almonds, squash cubes, apples, cinnamon, nutmeg, coconut sugar and milk, stir a bit, cover and cook on Low for 8 hours.
- Mash using a potato masher, divide into bowls and serve for breakfast.
- Enjoy!

Nutrition:

- Calories - 182
- Fat - 3
- Carbs - 14
- Protein - 2

VEGAN PUMPKIN SPICE SYRUP

Serving: 4

Ingredients:

- 2 cans full-fat coconut milk
- 2 cups packed light brown sugar
- 2 cups organic pumpkin puree
- 1 teaspoon ground cinnamon
- 1 teaspoon ground ginger
- ¼ teaspoon ground cardamom
- ¼ teaspoon ground allspice
- Pinch of cloves

Directions:

- In your slow cooker, combine the coconut milk, brown sugar, pumpkin puree , cinnamon, ground ginger, ground cardamom , ground allspice and cloves. Mix well with a whisk, and cook on LOW for 7 hours.
- When the cooking time is up, use a whisk to thoroughly mix all the ingredients and break the pieces that are still in the syrup.
- Keeps in the refrigerator for up to 1 week.

Nutrition:

- Calories - 33
- Fat - 0 g
- Carbs - 7 g
- Protein - 0 g

WATERMELON CHIA SMOOTHIE

Serving: 2

Ingredients:

- 2 slices lemon to garnish
- 1/3 cup water
- 3 cups watermelon cubes, deseeded
- 2 tablespoons chia seeds
- 2 sprigs minutes
- Ice cubes as needed

Directions:

- Add the ingredients one by one in your food processor or blender.
- Close the lid and blend to make a smooth mix.
- Add the prepare smoothie in tall serving glasses.
- Serve chilled. Garnish with mint leaves and a lemon slice.

Nutrition:

- Calories - 134
- Fat - 6g
- Carbs - 21.5g
- Sodium - 32mg

CLASSIC SLOW COOKED APPLE AND CINNAMON OATMEAL

Serving: 4

Ingredients:

- 2 small apples, peeled, cored, and chopped
- 2 cups of rolled oats
- 4 cups of milk
- 1 tablespoon ground cinnamon
- 4 tablespoons of brown sugar
- 1 pinch of salt
- 1/3 cup raisins or any dried fruit (optional

Directions:

- Place apples, oats, and milk into the crock-pot.
- Add brown sugar, cinnamon, and salt.
- Stir.
- Cook on HIGH for 1-2 hours or 2-3 hours on LOW.
- Always check consistency. Cook to your liking.
- Serve. Top with raisins or any dried fruit.
- (optional)

Nutrition:

- Calories - 300
- Fat - 1 g
- Carbs - 60 g
- Protein - 0 g

RASPBERRY MOUSSE

Serving: 2

Ingredients:

- 2 cups fresh raspberries
- ¼ cup swerve
- 1 cup unsweetened almond milk
- 3 tbsp whipped cream, sugar-free
- ¼ cup heavy cream
- Spices: ¼ tsp salt
- 1 tsp vanilla extract
- ¼ tsp ginger powder

Directions:

- Plug in the instant pot and press the "Saute" button. Place raspberries at the bottom of the inner pot and pour in ¼ cup of water. Add swerve and stir well. Cook for 10-12 minutes, stirring constantly.
- When most of the liquid has evaporated, pour in the milk and vanilla extract.
- Continue to cook for another 3-4 minutes.
- Stir in the whipped cream and heavy cream. Season with salt and ginger powder.
- Press the "Cancel" button and Chill well before serving.

Nutrition:

- Calories - 151
- Fat - 8.9g

- Carbs - 7.6g
- Protein - 2.3g

INSTANT POT HUEVOS RANCHEROS

Serving: 8

Ingredients:

- 1 tablespoon butter
- 10 eggs, beaten
- 1 cup light cream
- 8 ounces Mexican blend cheese, grated
- ½ teaspoon pepper
- ¼ teaspoon chili powder
- 1 clove of garlic, crushed
- 1 can green chilies, drained
- 8 tortillas
- 1 can red enchilada sauce

Directions:

- Grease the inside of the Instant Pot with butter.
- In a large bowl, mix together the eggs, cream, Mexican cheese, pepper, and chili powder. Stir in the garlic and chilies.
- Pour into the Instant Pot and close the lid. Press the Manual button and adjusts the cooking time to 15 minutes.
- Do natural pressure release.
- Assemble the dish by spooning the egg casserole to tortillas and serving with enchilada sauce.

Nutrition:

- Calories - 182
- Carbs - 4g
- Protein - 9g
- Fat - 14g

MUSTARD PORK WITH MUSHROOMS

Serving: 2

Ingredients:

- 10 oz pork, minced
- 6 oz button mushrooms, sliced
- 1 small zucchini, chopped
- 1 small onion, finely chopped
- 1 tbsp Dijon mustard
- 1 tbsp olive oil
- Spices: ¼ tsp dried basil, ground
- ¼ tsp garlic powder
- ½ tsp salt
- ½ tsp black pepper, ground

Directions:

- Plug in your instant pot and add the olive oil in the stainless steel insert. Press the "Saute" button and add onions. Stir-fry for 2-3 minutes and add minced pork. Sprinkle with garlic powder, salt, and pepper. Give it a good stir and cook for 3-4 minutes, or until browned.

- Add zucchini and mushrooms. Pour 1 cup of water and close the lid. Adjust the steam release handle and press the "MANUAL" button. Set the timer for 6 minutes and cook on "High" pressure.
- When you hear the cooker's end signal, perform a quick release of the pressure by turning the valve to the "Venting" position.
- Open the pot and press the "Saute" button.
- Stir in the Dijon mustard and sprinkle with dried thyme.

Nutrition:

- Calories - 312
- Fat - 12.7g
- Carbs - 6.4g
- Protein - 41.3g

HAM CASSEROLE

Serving: 2

Ingredients:

- 8 oz ham, chopped
- 4 oz Monterey Jack cheese, sliced
- ¼ cup heavy cream
- 1 teaspoon chili flakes
- 1 egg, beaten
- ½ teaspoon coconut oil

Directions:

- Brush the crockpot bottom with the coconut oil

- Then arrange the layer of ham and sprinkle it with chili flakes.
- After this, make the layer of sliced Monterey Jack cheese.
- In the separated bowl, mix up together heavy cream and egg.
- Pour the liquid over the cheese. Close the crockpot lid.
- Cook the casserole for 2.5 hours on High.

Nutrition:

- Calories - 490
- Fat - 35.8
- Carbs - 5.4
- Protein - 35.8

MEXICAN BREAKFAST

Serving: 5

Ingredients:

- 8 eggs, whisked
- 1 sweet potato, cubed
- 1 yellow onion, chopped
- ½ pound turkey bacon, cooked and crumbled
- 8 ounces mushrooms, chopped
- 1 red bell pepper, chopped
- Guacamole for serving
- Salsa for serving

Directions:

- In your slow cooker, mix eggs with sweet potato, onion, bacon, mushrooms and red bell pepper, stir a bit, cover and cook on Low for 6 hours.
- Divide between plates, top with guacamole and salsa and serve for breakfast.
- Enjoy!

Nutrition:

- Calories - 213
- Fat - 4
- Carbs - 12
- Protein - 4

YOGURT OATS MORNING

Serving: 2

Ingredients:

- 2/3 cup Greek yogurt
- 2/3 cup blueberries
- 2 tablespoons chia seeds
- 2/3 cup almond milk
- 2/3 cup old-fashioned oats
- 1/2 teaspoon vanilla
- 1 1/2 cup water
- 1 teaspoon sugar
- A pinch of cinnamon powder

Directions:

- In a heatproof bowl, mix the milk, yogurt, blueberries, oats, chia seeds, sugar, cinnamon, and vanilla.
- Take your 3-Quart Instant Pot; open the top lid. Plug it and turn it on.
- Pour the water and place steamer basket/trivet inside the pot; arrange the bowl over the basket/trivet.
- Close the top lid and seal its valve.
- Press "MANUAL" setting. Adjust cooking time to 6 minutes.
- Allow the recipe to cook for the set cooking time.
- After the set cooking time ends, press "CANCEL" and then press "QPR (Quick Pressure Release".
- Instant Pot will quickly release the pressure.
- Open the top lid, add the cooked recipe mix in serving plates.
- Serve and enjoy!

Nutrition:

- Calories - 239
- Fat - 6.5g
- Carbs - 38g
- Protein - 8g

LEEK AND TURKEY BREAKFAST MIX

Serving: 4

Ingredients:

- 2 cups leeks, chopped
- 2 tablespoons olive oil
- 1 cup mustard greens, torn
- 2 garlic cloves, minced
- 8 eggs, whisked
- 1 ½ cups turkey fillet, cooked and chopped

Directions:

- Heat up a pan with the oil over medium heat, add the turkey, stir, and let it brown for 5 minutes then Add the rest of the ingredients to the slow cooker as well, toss them to combine well, cover and cook on low for 7 hours.
- Divide everything between plates and serve for breakfast.

Nutrition:

- Calories - 281
- Fat - 16,2
- Carbs - 8,2
- Protein - 26

CINNAMON-RAISIN FRENCH TOAST BREAKFAST

Serving: 6

Ingredients:

- ½ cup packed light brown sugar
- 7 large eggs
- 16 cinnamon-raisin bread slices, cubed
- 1 cup heavy cream
- 2 ½ cups whole milk
- Non-stick cooking spray
- 2 cups pecans or walnuts (optional

Directions:

- Tightly line your slow cooker with foil and coat with non-stick spray.
- Pour the bread cubes into the prepared slow cooker.
- Whisk together the milk, eggs, cream, and sugar (2 cups of pecan or walnuts, optional).
- Pour the egg mixture over the bread in a slow cooker, and push down the bread a bit so it can soak in the egg.
- Cover and cook on LOW for 4 hours (or HIGH for 2 hours).
- Remove the top from the slow cooker, turn off the heat, and allow cooling for 15 minutes.
- Serve.

Nutrition:

- Calories - 149
- Fat - 7 g
- Carbs - 16 g
- Protein - 5 g

TAPIOCA BREAKFAST PUDDING

Serving: 4

Ingredients:

- ¼ cup tapioca pearls
- 20 ounces almond milk
- 1 teaspoon vanilla extract
- 1 tablespoon maple syrup

Directions:

- Combine all the ingredients in your slow cooker and cook on low heat for 5 hours.
- Stir the pudding, divide it into bowls and serve.

Nutrition:

- Calories - 376
- Fat - 33,8
- Carbs - 19,8
- Protein - 3,3

SWEET POTATO BACON AND EGG BREAKFAST

Serving: 4

Ingredients:

- 2 cups shredded sweet potatoes
- 5 slices of bacon, diced
- 8 eggs
- 1 cup shredded carrots
- ½ cup almond milk

Directions:

- Switch on your instant pot after placing it on a clean and dry kitchen platform. Press "Saute" cooking function.
- Open the pot lid; add and brown the bacon for about 2 minutes.
- Arrange a layer of potato hash on top. Arrange the carrots on top.
- Beat the eggs along with the milk in a mixing bowl. Add the mixture to the Instant Pot.
- Close the pot by closing the top lid. Also, ensure to seal the valve.
- Press "MANUAL" cooking function and set cooking time to 7 minutes. It will start cooking after a few minutes. Let the pot mix cook under pressure until the timer reads zero.
- Turn off and press "Cancel" cooking function. Quick release pressure.
- Open the pot and serve on a serving plate or bowl. Enjoy the Paleo dish!

Nutrition:

- Calories - 268
- Fat - 13.5g
- Carbs - 17.5g
- Protein - 17.5g

SPINACH TOMATO QUICHE

Serving: 4

Ingredients:

- 8 Eggs
- ⅓ cup Almond Milk
- 2 cups Baby Spinach, chopped
- 2 Green Onions, sliced
- 4 Tomato Slices, for topping
- 1 cup diced Tomato
- 1 teaspoon dried Basil
- 1 ½ cups Water

Directions:

- Grease a baking dish with cooking spray. Beat the eggs along with the milk and basil in a mixing bowl.
- Stir in the remaining ingredients. Pour the mixture into the dish.
- Switch on your instant pot after placing it on a clean and dry kitchen platform.
- Pour the water into the cooking pot area. Arrange the trivet inside it; arrange the dish over the trivet.

- Close the pot by closing the top lid. Also, ensure to seal the valve.
- Press "MANUAL" cooking function and set cooking time to 20 minutes. It will start cooking after a few minutes. Let the pot mix cook under pressure until the timer reads zero.
- Turn off and press "Cancel" cooking function. Quick release pressure.
- Open the pot and serve on a serving plate or bowl. Enjoy the Paleo dish!

Nutrition:

- Calories - 158
- Fat - 10g
- Carbs - 4g
- Protein - 13g

SPINACH AND HAM FRITTATA

Serving: 8

Ingredients:

- 8 eggs, beaten
- 2 cloves of garlic, minced
- 2 cups spinach, chopped
- 1 cup ham, diced
- 1 onion, chopped
- ½ cup coconut milk
- 1 teaspoon salt

Directions:

- Place all ingredients in the Instant Pot.
- Give a good stir.
- Close the lid and seal off the vents.
- Press the Manual button and adjust the cooking time to 10 minutes.
- Do natural pressure release.

Nutrition:

- Calories - 63
- Carbs - 5g
- Protein - 8g
- Fat - 3g

BEEF CASSEROLE

Serving: 4

Ingredients:

- 1 yellow onion, chopped
- 1 pound beef, cooked and chopped
- 1 red bell pepper, chopped
- 12 eggs, whisked
- 2 garlic cloves, minced
- 1 tablespoon olive oil
- 1 teaspoon fresh parsley, chopped
- 1 cup coconut milk
- A pinch of salt and black pepper

Directions:

- Grease the slow cooker with the olive oil then add the onion, beef, bell pepper, garlic, salt and pepper and toss.
- Add the eggs, parsley and the coconut milk over the beef mix, cover and cook on low for 8 hours.
- Divide everything between plates and serve for breakfast.

Nutrition:

- Calories - 590
- Fat - 38,1
- Carbs - 9,7
- Protein - 53,1

EASY IRISH OATMEAL

Serving: 3

Ingredients:

- 4 cups milk
- 1 ¾ cup steel-cut oats
- ½ cup dried cherries
- ½ cup maple syrup
- ½ teaspoon salt
- ¼ teaspoon ground allspice
- 4 cups water
- ½ cup blueberries
- 1/3 cup pecans, chopped

Directions:

- Place all ingredients except for the pecans in the Instant Pot.
- Give a good stir.
- Close the lid and seal off the vents.
- Press the Manual button and adjust the cooking time to 6 minutes.
- Do natural pressure release.
- Prior to serving, give the oatmeal and good stir.
- Garnish with pecans on top.

Nutrition:

- Calories - 597
- Carbs - 101.6g
- Protein - 21.4g
- Fat - 22.5g

GREAT VEGGIE BREAKFAST FRITTATA

Serving: 4

Ingredients:

- 6 eggs, whisked
- 4 ounces mushrooms, sliced
- ¼ cup spinach, chopped
- 2 green onions, chopped
- 1 teaspoon ghee
- ¼ cup cherry tomatoes, sliced
- 2 teaspoons Italian seasoning

Directions:

- Heat up a pan with the ghee over medium high heat, add mushrooms, onions, spinach, green onions and tomatoes, stir and cook for 2-3 minutes.
- Leave your frittata to cool down a bit, slice and serve.
- Enjoy!

Nutrition:

- Calories - 200
- Fat - 4
- Carbs - 12
- Protein - 3

VEGETABLES AND VEGAN

CARROTS AND TURNIPS

Serving: 2-4

Ingredients:

- 1 tbsp olive oil
- 1 small onion, chopped
- 3 medium carrots, sliced
- 2 medium turnips, peeled and sliced
- 1 tsp ground cu minutes
- 1 tsp lemon juice
- Salt and ground black pepper to the taste

- 1 cup water

Directions:

- Press the SAUTe button on the Instant Pot and heat the oil.
- Add the onion and saute for 2 minutes until fragrant.
- Add the carrots, turnips, cumin, and lemon juice.
- Saute for 1 minute more.
- Season with salt and pepper, stir well.
- Pour in the water. Close and lock the lid.
- Press the CANCEL key to stop the SAUTe function.
- Select MANUAL and cook at HIGH pressure for 7 minutes.
- Once timer goes off, use aQuick Release.
- Carefully unlock the lid.
- Taste for seasoning. Serve.

SWEET POTATO AND COCONUT CURRY

Serving: 3

Ingredients:

- 2 Tbsp olive oil
- 2 cloves garlic, crushed
- ½ tsp paprika
- 1 red chili, deseeded, sliced
- 4 1/2 oz red cabbage, shredded
- 5 1/3 oz passata
- 1 Tbsp peanut butter

- 1 large onion, halved, sliced
- 1 inch
- fresh ginger, peeled, grated
- ¼ tsp cayenne
- 1 red pepper, deseeded, sliced
- 1 oz sweet potatoes
- 6 3/4 oz coconut milk
- To serve: Cooked couscous to serve
- A handful fresh cilantro, chopped

Directions:

- Place a skillet over medium heat. Add ½ Tbsp oil and heat. Add onion and saute until Add ginger and garlic and saute for 10-15 seconds. Add cayenne pepper and paprika and cook for a minute. Place the skillet back over heat. Add ½ Tbsp oil and heat. Add red pepper, red chili and paprika and cook for 10-15 seconds.
- Add cabbage and cook for a couple of minutes. Place the skillet back over heat. Add remaining oil and heat. Add sweet potatoes and cook until the edges are light brown. Add passata and coconut milk into the slow cooker and mix the entire ingredients in the slow cooker until well combined.
- Cover and cook for 6 to 8 hours on low or until the sweet potatoes are cooked.
- Add peanut butter and stir. Add salt and pepper to taste.
- Serve over couscous. Garnish with cilantro and serve.

Nutrition:

- Calories - 434

CROCK POT BBQ VEGETABLE LASAGNA

Serving: 8

Ingredients:

- 2 large eggplants, sliced into long noodles
- 1 large onion, chopped
- 2 cloves garlic, crushed
- 1 cup cottage cheese
- 1 cup mozzarella cheese
- 1 cup keto BBQ sauce
- Salt and pepper to taste
- For BBQ Sauce: ½ cup sugar-free ketchup
- 1 tablespoon hot sauce
- 1 tablespoon mustard
- 1 teaspoon liquid smoke
- 1 teaspoon Worcestershire
- ½ teaspoon chili powder
- ½ teaspoon cu minutes
- ¼ teaspoon cayenne pepper
- ½ teaspoon salt
- For garnishing: 1 teaspoon red pepper flakes
- Fresh parsley

Directions:

- BBQ sauce: Blend all the ingredients in a bowl.

- Lasagna: Lay the eggplant noodles down flat in the crock pot.
- Layer the BBQ sauce, onion, garlic, mozzarella cheese and cottage cheese.
- Repeat to make three layers with eggplant, sauce, veggies and cheese.
- Add a final fourth layer of eggplant, topped with a generous amount of sauce.
- Season with some salt and pepper.
- Cover and cook on high for 3-4 hours.
- Sprinkle some mozzarella cheese and cook for an additional 20-30 minutes.
- Garnish with some red pepper flakes and fresh parsley.
- Serve hot.

Nutrition:

- Calories - 223
- Fat - 14 g
- Carbs - 5 g
- Protein - 20 g

POTATOES AU GRATIN

Serving: 4-6

Ingredients:

- 2 tbsp butter
- ½ cup yellow onion, chopped
- 1 cup chicken stock
- 6 potatoes, peeled and sliced
- ½ cup sour cream

- 1 cup Monterey jack cheese, shredded
- Salt and ground black pepper to taste
- For the topping: 1 cup bread crumbs
- 3 tbsp melted butter

Directions:

- To preheat the Instant Pot, select SAUTe. Once hot, add the butter and melt it.
- Add the onion and saute for about 5 minutes, until softened.
- Pour in the stock and put a steam rack in the pot.
- Place the potatoes on the rack. Close and lock the lid.
- Press the CANCEL button to stop the SAUTE function, then select the MANUAL setting and set the cooking time for 5 minutes at HIGH pressure.
- In a small bowl, combine the bread crumbs and 3 tablespoon butter.
- Mix well.
- When the timer goes off, use aQuick Release.
- Carefully open the lid.
- Remove the potatoes and steam rack from the pot.
- Add the cream and cheese to the pot and stir well. Return the potatoes, season with salt and pepper and gently stir.
- Preheat the oven to broil.
- Pour the mixture in a baking dish, top with bread crumbs mix and broil for 7 minutes.
- Serve.

COLORFUL VEGETABLE RISOTTO

Serving: 4

Ingredients:

- 1 tablespoon olive oil
- ¼ cup shallots, diced
- 2 cloves garlic, crushed and minced
- 1 cup short grain brown rice
- ¼ cup dry white wine
- 2 cups vegetable stock
- ½ cup carrots, shredded
- ½ cup zucchini, shredded (excess liquid removed
- ½ cup yellow bell pepper, diced
- ½ teaspoon salt
- 1 teaspoon black pepper
- 2 teaspoons fresh tarragon
- 1 cup various colored grape tomatoes, quartered
- ½ cup fresh peas
- 1 tablespoon fresh chives
- ¼ cup fresh parsley
- ¼ cup shredded Asiago cheese

Directions:

- Heat the olive oil in a skillet over medium heat.
- Add the shallots and garlic. Saute until Add the brown rice and cook, stirring frequently for 2-3 minutes, or until lightly toasted.
- Add the wine and cook, while stirring, until the wine has evaporated.

- Remove the pan from the heat and To the slow cooker, add the carrots, zucchini, and bell pepper. Season the vegetables and rice with salt, black pepper, and tarragon. Mix well.
- Add the vegetable stock and stir.
- Cover and cook on HIGH for 2 ½ hours.
- Remove the lid and stir in the tomatoes, peas, chives, parsley and Asiago cheese.
- Cover and cook an additional 20 minutes before serving.

Nutrition:

- Calories - 138
- Fat - 4 g
- Carbs - 20 g
- Protein - 3 g

CROCK POT SUMMER VEGGIES

Serving: 6

Ingredients:

- 2 cups chicken or vegetable stock
- 3 cups cauliflower, small florets
- 2 cups kale, chopped
- 1 large onion, chopped
- 1 cup heavy cream
- 2 teaspoons coriander
- 2 teaspoons cu minutes
- 1½ teaspoons paprika
- ½ teaspoon cardamom
- ¼ teaspoon nutmeg

- ½ teaspoon cayenne pepper
- ¼ cup tomato paste
- 1 tablespoon garlic, chopped
- 1 tablespoon fresh ginger, minced
- 1 tablespoon butter
- ½ teaspoon freshly ground pepper
- 1½ teaspoons salt
- ½ cup fresh cilantro, finely chopped

Directions:

- Preheat the crock pot over medium-high heat. Add butter.
- Cook the onion, ginger and garlic until golden brown.
- Add all the spices.
- Cook for about 3 minutes to toast the spices.
- Add in the tomato paste, stock and cream. Stir until well combined.
- Now add the vegetables.
- Cover and cook for about 3-4 hours on low.
- Garnish with some fresh cilantro and serve warm.

Nutrition:

- Calories - 287
- Fat - 14.4 g
- Protein - 35.6 g

SUMMERY VEGGIE CURRY

Serving: 3

Ingredients:

- For Spice Mixture: 1 tbsp. coriander seeds
- ½ tsp cumin seeds
- ½ tsp mustard seeds
- 2 tbsp. coconut shreds
- 2 tbsp. chopped peanuts
- 3 chopped garlic cloves
- 1 chopped hot green chile, chopped
- ½ tsp cayenne pepper
- ½ tsp ground turmeric
- Salt, to taste
- 1 tsp fresh lemon juice
- 1 cup plus 2 tsp water (divided)
- 6 baby eggplants

Directions:

- Heat a non-stick frying pan over medium heat and saute coriander, cumin and mustard seeds for about 2 minutes.
- Add the coconut and peanuts and saute for about 1-2 minutes.
- Remove from heat and keep aside to cool slightly.
- In a small food processor, add coconut mixture, garlic, chile, spices, lemon juice and 2 teaspoons of water and pulse until a coarse mixture is formed.

- Carefully, make cross cuts on each eggplant, not all the way through.
- Fill the spice mixture into the crosscut.
- In the pot of Instant Pot, place the eggplants and with 1 cup of water and ¼ teaspoon of salt.
- Secure the lid and place the pressure valve to "Seal" position.
- Select "MANUAL" and cook under "High Pressure" for about 5 minutes.
- Select the "Cancel" and carefully do a "Natural" release.
- Remove the lid and serve.

Nutrition:

- Calories - 96
- Fat - 4.4g
- Carbs - 4.3g
- Protein - 4.1g

SOUTH-EAST ASIAN CURRY

Serving: 4

Ingredients:

- 3 cups sliced fresh mushrooms
- ½ tsp minced garlic
- Salt, to taste
- ¼ tsp ground coriander
- ¼ tsp ground cu minutes
- ¼ tsp ground turmeric
- ¼ tsp red chili powder
- ½ cup unsweetened coconut milk

- ¼ cup plain Greek yogurt

Directions:

- In a Pyrex dish that will fit in an Instant Pot, add all ingredients and stir to combine.
- In the bottom of Instant Pot, arrange a steamer trivet and pour 1 cup of water.
- Place the Pyrex dish on top of the trivet.
- Secure the lid and place the pressure valve to "Seal" position.
- Select "MANUAL" and cook under "High Pressure" for about 27 minutes.
- Select the "Cancel" and carefully do a "Natural" release.
- Remove the lid and serve.

Nutrition:

- Calories - 93
- Fat - 7.6g
- Carbs - 2.22g
- Protein - 3.3g

CELERY SPINACH STEW

Serving: 4

Ingredients:

- 2 cups fresh spinach; chopped
- 1 cup celery leaves; chopped.
- 2 cups heavy cream
- 1 tablespoon lemon juice

- 1 small onion; chopped.
- 2 tablespoon butter
- 1 cup celery stalks; chopped.
- 2 garlic cloves; minced
- 1/2 teaspoon black pepper; ground.
- 1 tablespoon fresh mint; torn
- 1 teaspoon salt

Directions:

- In a large colander, combine spinach and celery. Rinse well under running water and drain. a
- cutting board cut into bite-sized pieces, Set aside.
- Plug in your instant pot and press the "SAUTE" button. Add butter and stir constantly until melts.
- Add celery stalks, garlic, and onions. Cook for 2 minutes and add celery leaves and spinach. Sprinkle with salt and pepper. Cook for 2-3 minutes and pour in the heavy cream.
- Securely lock the lid and press the "MANUAL" button. Adjust the steam release handle and set the timer for 5 minutes. Cook on "HIGH" pressure.
- When you hear the cooker's end signal, perform a quick release of the pressure and open the pot.
- Stir in the mint and lemon juice. Let it chill for 5 minutes before serving

Nutrition:

- Calories - 278
- Fat - 28.2g
- Carbs - 4.3g
- Protein - 2.3g

CREAMY SPINACH BALLS

Serving: 5

Ingredients:

- 7-ounce spinach; finely chopped
- 1 large tomato; sliced
- 5 large eggs
- 1/2 cup almond flour
- 1 cup cream cheese
- 1/4 cup Feta cheese
- 1/4 cup shredded mozzarella
- 3 tablespoon butter; melted
- 2 tablespoon olive oil
- 2 tablespoon heavy cream
- 1 teaspoon garlic powder
- 1/2 teaspoon dried oregano
- 1/4 teaspoon dried thyme
- 1/2 teaspoon salt

Directions:

- In a large bowl, combine together spinach, cheese, eggs, melted butter, and almond flour. Season with salt, thyme, oregano, and garlic powder.
- Mix well and shape 10 equal balls. If the mixture is too sticky, add some more almond flour.
- Coat a small oven-safe bowl with olive oil and add a layer of sliced tomatoes. Gently place the balls on top and tightly wrap with aluminum foil.

- Plug in the instant pot and position a trivet at the bottom of the inner pot. Pour in one cup of water and place the bowl on the trivet.
- Seal the lid and set the steam release handle to the "SEALING" position. Press the "MANUAL" button and set the timer for 8 minutes on high pressure.
- When done, perform a quick pressure release and open the lid. Carefully remove the bowl from the pot and chill for a while. Optionally, top with some Greek yogurt before serving

Nutrition:

- Calories - 420
- Fat - 39.3g
- Carbs - 4g
- Protein - 13.5g

SWEET POTATO SPICY CURRY STEW

Serving: 4-6

Ingredients:

- 1 onion, diced
- 2 teaspoons fresh ginger, peeled and grated
- 2 cloves garlic, minced
- 2 small sweet potatoes, peeled and diced into chunks
- 1 leek, clean, trimmed and sliced finely
- 2 ¼ cups full-fat coconut milk
- 2 ½ tablespoons lime juice

- ½ -1 teaspoon red pepper flakes, (or to taste
- cilantro, chopped, for the garnish
- Lime, thinly sliced, for the garnish (optional)
- For the spicy paste
- 1 tablespoon coconut oil
- 2 teaspoons curry powder
- 1 teaspoon turmeric
- 1 teaspoon sea salt
- 2 tablespoons Thai red curry paste
- 3 medium tomatoes, diced

Directions:

- Place the onion, ginger, garlic, sweet potatoes, zucchini and red bell pepper into the slow cooker
- In a bowl, combine the ingredients for the spice paste. Pour over the vegetables.
- Add the coconut milk.
- Cook for 4 hours on LOW or until sweet potatoes are tender.
- Stir in the lime juice and red pepper flakes. Adjust the flavor with more salt, if needed.
- Garnish with chopped cilantro, if desired, and serve.

Nutrition:

- Calories - 266
- Fat - 20.2 g
- Carbs - 20.6 g
- Protein - 2.6 g

BUTTERY MUSHROOM RICE

Serving: 4

Ingredients:

- ½ pound mushrooms, sliced
- 2 tablespoons vegan butter
- 1 onion, diced
- 3 cloves garlic
- 1 teaspoon thyme
- 1 cup rice, white
- 2 cups vegetable broth
- ½ cup vegan Parmesan

Directions:

- Add all ingredients to the slow cooker and cook covered on low for 6 hours or on high for half that time.

Nutrition:

- Calories - 297
- Fat - 10 g
- Carbs - 43 g
- Protein - 7 g

QUICK CORN ON THE COB

Serving: 4

Ingredients:

- 4 ears fresh corn

Directions:

- Pour water into Instant Pot. Place steamer basket over water and arrange corn in the basket.
- Close lid and set cooking time to 3 minutes. Use the quick pressure release method to release steam. Serve corn hot with butter and salt.

Nutrition:

- Calories - 88
- Fat - 1.38 g
- Carbs - 19.07 g
- Protein - 3.34 g

GINGERBREAD LATTE

Serving: 8

Ingredients:

- 6-8 cups coconut milk (decide based on how strong you like your lattes
- ¼ cup maple syrup (or molasses)
- 2 teaspoons cinnamon, ground
- 1 teaspoon ginger, ground

- ½ teaspoon nutmeg, ground
- ½ teaspoon cloves, ground
- 3 cups brewed coffee
- 1 teaspoon vanilla extract
- Optional: ⅓ cup pumpkin puree
- Coconut whipped cream

Directions:

- Combine all ingredients in the slow cooker and cook on low, covered, for 2-3 hours. Make sure it doesn't boil. You can then leave the latte on warm setting for 2 hours.
- Serve warm topped with whipped cream and a dusting of cinnamon.

Nutrition:

- Calories - 365
- Fat - 36 g
- Carbs - 12 g
- Protein - 4 g

CREAM CHEESE RED POTATO

Serving: 2

Ingredients:

- 1 pound red potatoes, quartered
- 4 ounces cream cheese
- 1 (4.5 ounce) can cream of potato soup
- 1 envelope ranch salad dressing mix

Directions:

- Place the potatoes in a 2-quart slow cooker.
- In a mixing bowl, combine the cream cheese, soup, and salad dressing mix. Beat it all together.
- Add the sauce to the slow cooker and stir well to combine.
- Cover, and cook for 8 hours on LOW. The potatoes should be fork tender.

Nutrition:

- Calories - 309
- Fat - 15 g
- Carbs - 38 g
- Protein - 7 g

TOMATO EGGPLANT STEW

Serving: 2

Ingredients:

- 1 small eggplant, roughly chopped
- 12 ounces canned tomatoes, chopped
- 1 small red onion, chopped
- ½ tablespoon smoked paprika
- 1 teaspoon ground cu minutes
- 1 cup veggie stock
- Salt and pepper to taste

Directions:

- In the slow cooker, combine all the ingredients, and stir to combine.
- Cook on LOW for 8 hours.
- Serve hot!

Nutrition:

- Calories - 261
- Fat - 4.2 g
- Carbs - 14 g
- Protein - 7 g

SLOW COOKER ALMOND QUINOA CURRY

Serving: 4

Ingredients:

- 1 cup water
- ½ medium sweet potato, peeled and chopped
- ½ large head of broccoli, cut into florets
- ¼ white onion, diced
- ½ (15-ounce can organic chickpeas, drained and rinsed
- ½ (28-ounce) can diced tomatoes
- 1 (14.5-ounce) can almond milk
- 2 tablespoons quinoa
- 1 garlic cloves, minced
- 1 tablespoon freshly grated ginger
- 1 tablespoon freshly grated turmeric
- 1 teaspoon wheat-free tamari sauce

- ½ teaspoon miso (or additional tamari)
- ¼ teaspoon chili flakes

Directions:

- Combine all the ingredients in a slow cooker. Stir until everything is fully incorporated.
- Turn the slow cooker to HIGH and cook for 3-4 hours, until sweet potato cooks through and the curry has thickened.

Nutrition:

- Calories - 507
- Fat - 32 g
- Carbs - 50 g
- Protein - 13 g

GREENS IN CAYENNE SAUCE

Serving: 3

Ingredients:

- 1 cup broccoli; sliced
- 1 tablespoon lime juice; freshly squeezed
- 1 tablespoon butter
- 1 cup cauliflower
- 1 cup sour cream
- 2 garlic cloves; peeled
- 2 large eggs
- 1/4 teaspoon dried oregano; ground.
- 1 teaspoon onion powder
- 1 teaspoon cayenne pepper; ground.

- 1 teaspoon sea salt

Directions:

- In a food processor, combine sour cream, garlic, eggs, lime juice, onion powder, cayenne pepper, oregano, and salt. Pulse until well incorporated and set aside.
- Plug in the instant pot and place the butter in the stainless steel insert. Press the "SAUTE" button and gently stir until melts.
- Add broccoli and cauliflower. Sprinkle with a pinch of salt and cook for 5 minutes, stirring occasionally Remove the vegetables to a bowl and cover with a lid
- Now; pour in the blended mixture and close the lid. Adjust the steam release handle and press the "MANUAL" button. Set the timer for 3 minutes and cook on "HIGH" pressure.
- When you hear the cooker's end signal, perform a quick pressure release and open the pot
- Drizzle the broccoli and cauliflower with sauce and give it a good stir. a
- serving plate and enjoy!

Nutrition:

- Calories - 272
- Fat - 23.5g
- Carbs - 7.1g
- Protein - 8.5g

CHESSY CANNELLONI EGGPLANT

Serving: 5

Ingredients:

- 1 small eggplant; sliced lengthwise
- 3 tablespoon oil
- 1 small chili pepper; sliced
- 1 onion; finely chopped
- 4 tablespoon cottage cheese
- 3 tablespoon Feta cheese
- 2 tablespoon sour cream
- 1 cup cherry tomatoes; whole
- 1/4 teaspoon dried thyme
- 1/2 teaspoon dried oregano
- 1 teaspoon salt

Directions:

- In a small bowl, combine together cottage cheese, Feta cheese, and sour cream. Sprinkle with some dried thyme and set aside.
- Slice eggplants lengthwise into about 1/4-inch-thick slices. Sprinkle with some salt and set aside for ten minutes.
- Meanwhile, plug in the instant pot and grease the inner pot with oil. Add onions and chili pepper. Sprinkle with some more salt and saute for 3-4 minutes. Now add tomatoes and continue to cook until soft. If necessary, add 2-3 tablespoon of water. Remove from the pot and set aside
- Now rinse well the eggplants and gently squeeze with your hands, Set aside.

- Line s small baking pan with some parchment paper and add the tomato sauce. Place eggplant slices, one at the time, and spread about two tablespoons of the cheese mixture on each. Gently roll up and secure with toothpicks. Repeat the process with the remaining eggplant slices and loosely cover with some aluminum foil.
- Position a trivet at the bottom of the instant pot and place the pan on top. Pour in one cup of water. Seal the lid and set the steam release handle to the "SEALING" position.
- Press the "MANUAL" button and set the timer for 13 minutes on high pressure.
- When done; perform a quick pressure release and open the lid. Remove the pan from the pot and chill for a while
- Sprinkle with some Parmesan before serving.

Nutrition:

- Calories - 146
- Fat - 10.9g
- Carbs - 5.6g
- Protein - 4g

LEEK SWISS CHARD STIRFRY

Serving: 4

Ingredients:

- 2 cups Swiss chard; chopped
- 2 cups leeks; chopped
- 1 tablespoon olive oil

- 1 small onion; chopped
- 2 garlic cloves; finely chopped
- 1/2 cup cream cheese; full-fat
- 2 tablespoon Parmesan cheese; grated
- 1/4 teaspoon cayenne pepper; ground.
- 1/2 teaspoon black pepper; ground.
- 1 teaspoon pink Himalayan salt

Directions:

- In a large colander, combine Swiss chard and leek. Rinse under cold running water and drain. Chop into small pieces and set aside.
- Plug in the instant pot and add olive oil to the stainless steel insert. Press the "SAUTE" button and add onions and garlic. Cook for 5 minutes, or until the onions Now; add greens and sprinkle with salt, pepper, and cayenne pepper. Stir-fry for 10-12 minutes
- Stir in the cream cheese and sprinkle all with parmesan. Continue to cook for 2-3 minutes more, stirring occasionally.

Nutrition:

- Calories - 195
- Fat - 15.4g
- Carbs - 8.81g
- Protein - 5.8g

SOUPS AND STEWS

CHANAFLOWER MASALA

Serving: 4

Ingredients:

- 2 cups chopped raw cauliflower
- 1 can chopped tomatoes
- 1 cup water
- 1 onion, minced
- 4 tbsp. chana masala mix
- 1 tbsp. oil
- salt and pepper

Directions:

- Warm the oil in your Instant Pot.
- Soften the onion 5 minutes.
- Mix all the ingredients in your Instant Pot.
- Seal and cook on Stew for 10 minutes.
- Release the pressure quickly and stir well.
- Rest before serving.

Nutrition:

- Calories - 100
- Fat - 5.5g
- Carbs - 10g
- Protein - 2g

FALL-WEATHER SOUP

Serving: 8

Ingredients:

- 3 tbsp. butter
- 1 peeled and chopped carrot
- 1 chopped small yellow onion
- 8 cups small cauliflower florets
- 4 cups homemade vegetable broth
- 1 cup shredded sharp cheddar cheese
- ½ cup heavy cream
- Salt and freshly ground black pepper, to taste

Directions:

- Place the oil and butter in the Instant Pot and select "Saute". Then add the carrot and onion and cook for about 5 minutes.
- Select the "Cancel" and stir in the cauliflower and broth.
- Secure the lid and place the pressure valve to "Seal" position.
- Select "MANUAL" and cook under "High Pressure" for about 5 minutes.
- Select the "Cancel" and carefully do a "Quick" release.
- Remove the lid and with and with an immersion blender, puree the soup.
- Select "Saute" and stir in remaining ingredients.
- Cook for about 2-3 minutes.
- Select the "Cancel" and serve hot.

Nutrition:

- Calories - 172
- Fat - 12.6g
- Carbs - 0.96g
- Protein - 8.3g

SPICY CHIPOTLE SHORT RIBS STEW

Serving: 6

Ingredients:

- For stew: 2 lbs beef short ribs
- 2 cups tomatoes, chopped
- 1 cup white onions, chopped
- 3 Poblano peppers, cut into strips
- 2 chipotle peppers, finely chopped
- 3 tbsp olive oil
- 3 cups beef broth
- Spices: 1 tsp salt
- ½ tsp white pepper, freshly ground

Directions:

- Rub the meat with salt and pepper.
- Set aside.
- Plug in the instant pot and grease the inner pot with olive oil. Press the "Saute" button and add peppers, tomatoes, and onions.
- Cook for 15 minutes, stirring occasionally.
- Now, pour in the broth and add the meat. Securely lock the lid and set the steam release

handle to the "Sealing" position. Press the "MANUAL" button and set the timer for 35 minutes on high pressure.
- When you hear the end signal, perform a quick pressure release and open the lid.
- Serve warm.

Nutrition:

- Calories - 423
- Fat - 21.5g
- Carbs - 6.4g
- Protein - 47.6g

BEEF STEWED IN SATAY SAUCE

Serving: 4

Ingredients:

- 1lb cubed stewing beef
- 3 chopped carrots
- 3 chopped onions
- 7oz peanut butter
- 6oz coconut cream
- 2 tbsp. lemon juice
- 2 tbsp. grated ginger
- 1 tbsp. chili paste
- 1 tbsp. cu minutes
- salt and pepper

Directions:

- Heat your Instant Pot up with the peanut butter and coconut.
- Stir until melted.
- Add the remaining spices and keep stirring.
- Turn down to low. Add all other ingredients.
- Cook for 20 minutes on Stew.

Nutrition:

- Calories - 380
- Fat - 30g
- Carbs - 6g
- Protein - 27g

JALAPENO CHILI

Serving: 4

Ingredients:

- For chili: 1 lb ground beef
- 3 jalapeno peppers
- 1 large onion, chopped
- 2 garlic cloves, crushed
- 3 cups beef broth
- 3 tbsp oil
- 3 tbsp butter
- Spices: ½ tsp salt
- 1 tsp ground cu minutes
- ½ tsp chili powder

Directions:

- Take a sharp knife and slice each pepper down the middle. Make sure you cut them in two equal halves so the seeds and the stems can be removed easily.
- Place them in a small saucepan along with salt, cumin, and chili powder. Drizzle with oil and heat up. Cook for 2-3 minutes and then add onions. Continue to cook for another 2-3 minutes. Remove from the heat and Add the meat and garlic. Pour in the broth and stir well. Seal the lid and set the steam release handle to the "Sealing" position.
- Press the "Meat" button,
- When done, release the pressure naturally for 10-15 minutes and then move the pressure valve to the "Venting" position to release the remaining pressure.
- Carefully open the lid and stir in the butter. Chill for a while and serve.
- Optionally, sprinkle with grated Parmesan cheese before serving.

Nutrition:

- Calories - 428
- Fat - 27.2g
- Carbs - 4.4g
- Protein - 38.8g

ITALIAN MEATBALL SOUP

Serving: 2

Ingredients:

- 3 medium carrots, sliced
- 2 ribs celery, sliced
- 1 medium yellow onion, diced
- 1 teaspoon dried Italian seasoning
- ¼ teaspoon black pepper
- 1 bay leaf
- 12 ounces frozen Italian meatballs (the fully cooked kind
- 4 cups beef broth
- 2 cups water
- ⅝ cup dry red wine
- 2 (15-ounce) cans diced tomatoes with Italian seasoning
- ¾ cup dry ditalini pasta (any small pasta will do)
- 3-5 ounces fresh baby spinach
- Freshly grated Parmesan cheese, for serving

Directions:

- Place all ingredients except for the pasta and spinach in the slow cooker.
- Cook on low for 6 hours.
- Add the pasta and baby spinach and cook for an additional 30 minutes or until pasta is tender.
- Serve with grated parmesan.

Nutrition:

- Calories - 170
- Fat - 7 g
- Carbs - 13 g
- Protein - 9 g

SQUASH CHICKEN MUSHROOM SOUP

Serving: 4

Ingredients:

- 2 cups chopped mushrooms
- 1 yellow summer squash, chopped
- 1 pound boneless, skinless chicken breast, make large chunks
- 2 ½ cups chicken broth
- 1 onion, make thin slices
- 3 garlic cloves, minced
- 1 teaspoon salt
- 1 teaspoon Italian seasoning or poultry seasoning
- 1 teaspoon (ground black pepper
- 1 cup heavy (whipping) cream

Directions:

- Take your Instant Pot; open the top lid. Plug it and turn it on.
- In the cooking pot area, add the onion, garlic, mushrooms, squash, chicken, chicken broth, salt, pepper, and Italian seasoning. Using a spatula, stir the ingredients.

- Close the top lid and seal its valve.
- Press "MANUAL" setting. Adjust cooking time to 15 minutes.
- Allow the recipe to cook for the set cooking time.
- After the set cooking time ends, press "CANCEL" and then press "NPR (Natural Pressure Release)".
- Instant Pot will slowly and naturally release the pressure.
- Unlock the lid; Using an immersion blender, puree the vegetables.
- Shred the chicken and stir it back into the soup. Add the cream and stir well.
- Serve warm.

Nutrition:

- Calories - 387
- Fat - 28g
- Carbs - 12g
- Protein - 31g

CHICKEN STEW WITH MUSHROOMS

Serving: 4

Ingredients:

- 1 lb. turkey breast, boneless, skinless and chopped into bite-sized pieces
- 1 lb. chicken breast, boneless, skinless, and chopped into bite-sized pieces
- 12 oz. button mushrooms, sliced

- 2 tbsp. butter, softened
- 1 tbsp. olive oil
- A bunch of celery leaves, finely chopped
- Spices: 1 tsp salt
- ½ tsp freshly ground pepper
- 1 tbsp. cayenne pepper

Directions:

- Plug in your instant pot and grease the bottom of the stainless steel insert with one tablespoon of olive oil. Now, add turkey breast, salt, pepper, and cayenne pepper. Give it a good stir, add two cups of water, and close the lid. Set the steam release handle and press "Meat" button. Cook for 13 minutes and release the steam handle.
- Uncover and add chicken breast, butter, and one more cup of water. Continue to simmer for 15 minutes more, or until the meat is fully cooked and tender.
- Finally, add mushrooms and celery leaves. I personally don't like to overcook the mushrooms so about 10 minutes in the pot will be more than enough.
- Serve warm.

Nutrition:

- Calories - 436
- Fat - 20.5g
- Carbs - 2.8g
- Protein - 57g

CREAMY THAI COCONUT CHICKEN SOUP

Serving: 4

Ingredients:

- 2 tablespoons oil
- 1 onion, quartered
- 2 pounds chicken breasts, skin and bones removed
- 2 tablespoons Thai red curry paste
- 1 red bell pepper, cut into strips
- 6 slices galangal or ginger
- 6 kaffir lime leaves
- 3 cups chicken broth
- 2 tablespoons fish sauce
- 1 tablespoon sugar
- ¾ cup coconut milk
- 2 ½ tablespoons lime juice
- Cilantro leaves for serving

Directions:

- Press the Saute button on the Instant Pot.
- Heat the oil and saute the onion and chicken. Turn the chicken constantly until slightly golden.
- Add the red curry paste, bell pepper, galangal, and kaffir limes.
- After 30 seconds, add the chicken broth, fish sauce, and sugar.
- Close the lid and press the Manual button.
- Adjust the cooking button to 15 minutes.
- Do quick pressure release.

- Once the lid is open, press the Saute button and add the coconut milk and lime juice.
- Allow simmering for 5 more minutes.
- Serve with cilantro leaves.

Nutrition:

- Calories - 624
- Carbs - 17.8g
- Protein - 52.6g
- Fat - 39.1g

SWISS CHARD STEM SOUP

Serving: 6

Ingredients:

- 8 cups Swiss Chard stems, diced
- 3 leeks, chopped
- 1 celeriac, peeled and diced
- 1 potato, peeled and diced
- 1 ½ cups chicken stock
- 1 cup coconut milk
- Salt and pepper to taste

Directions:

- Place all ingredients in the Instant Pot.
- Give a good stir to combine everything.
- Close the lid and press the Manual button.
- Adjust the cooking time to 4 minutes.
- Do natural pressure release.

Nutrition:

- Calories - 200
- Carbs - 23.9g
- Protein - 5.4g
- Fat - 10.6g

SICHUAN PORK SOUP

Serving: 6

Ingredients:

- 2 tablespoons olive oil
- 1 tablespoon minced garlic
- 2 tablespoons soy sauce
- 2 tablespoons black vinegar
- 1 teaspoons Truvia
- 2 teaspoons Sichuan peppercorns, crushed
- 1 to 2 teaspoons salt
- ½ onion, sliced
- 1-pound pork shoulder, cut into 2-inch chunks
- 2 tablespoons doubanjiang
- 3 cups water
- 3 to 4 cups chopped bok choy
- ¼ cup chopped fresh cilantro

Directions:

- Select "Saute" to preheat the Instant Pot and adjust to high heat. When the hot, add oil and let it shimmer. Add the garlic and ginger and saute for 1 to 2 minutes.

- Add the soy sauce, vinegar, sweetener, peppercorns, salt, onion, pork, doubanjiang, and water. Stir well.
- Latch the lid. Select "Pressure Cook" or "MANUAL" and set pressure to high and cook for 20 minutes. After the time finishes, allow 10 minutes to naturally release the pressure. For any remaining pressure, just quick-release it. Open the lid.
- Open the pot and add the bok choy. Close the lid and let it cook in the residual heat for about 10 minutes, or until softened, but not mushy.
- Ladle the soup into bowls and top with the cilantro. Serve and enjoy!

Nutrition:

- Calories - 256
- Fat - 20.0g
- Protein - 14.0g
- Carbs - 5.0g
- Carbs - - 4.0g
- Sugar - 2.0g

VICHYSSOISE

Serving: 4

Ingredients:

- For soup: 2 cups cauliflower, chopped
- 1 large leek, chopped
- 1 small onion, finely chopped
- 1 cup cream cheese

- 5 cups vegetable stock
- 3 tbsp butter
- 1 tsp lemon juice, freshly squeezed
- Spices: 1/8 tsp nutmeg
- ¼ tsp dried parsley
- 1 bay leaf
- ½ tsp salt
- ¼ tsp white pepper, freshly ground
- Freshly snipped chives, optional

Directions:

- Plug in your instant pot and press the "Saute" button. Melt the butter in the stainless steel insert and add the leeks and onions.
- Stir-fry for about 4-5 minutes without browning.
- Add the cauliflower, vegetable stock, lemon juice, nutmeg, parsley, and bay leaf. Sprinkle with salt and pepper and securely lock the lid. Press the "MANUAL" button and set the timer for 10 minutes.
- Cook on high pressure.
- When done, press the "Cancel" button and move the pressure valve to the "Venting" position to release thepressure.Remove and discard the bay leaf and pour the soup through a large sieve. Alternatively, Pour the soup back to the pot and press the "Saute" button. Stir in the cream cheese and optionally sprinkle with some more salt or pepper to taste.
- Cook for another 5 minutes, stirring constantly.
- Press the "Cancel" button to turn off the pot. Serve immediately.

Nutrition:

- Calories - 320
- Fat - 29.1g
- Carbs - 7.4g
- Protein - 6.5g

NACHO CHEESE CHICKEN CHOWDER

Serving: 6

Ingredients:

- 1 pound skinless, boneless chicken breast halves, cut into ½-inch strips
- 2 14 ½-ounce cans Mexican-style stewed tomatoes, undrained
- 1 10¾-ounce can condensed nacho cheese soup
- 2 cups frozen whole kernel corn
- Shredded cheddar cheese

Directions:

- Stir chicken, undrained tomatoes, soup, and corn together.
- Cover and cook for 4 to 5 hours on LOW or for 2 to 2 ½ hours on HIGH.
- Serve sprinkled with cheese.

Nutrition:

- Calories - 244
- Fat - 6 g

- Carbs - 24 g
- Protein - 23 g

BEEF STEW WITH EGGPLANTS

Serving: 6

Ingredients:

- For stew: 2 lbs beef stew meat
- 1 cup eggplant, cut into chunks
- 6 bacon slices
- 1 cup cherry tomatoes, chopped
- 1 large onion, finely chopped
- 3 garlic cloves, crushed
- 4 cups beef broth
- 4 tbsp butter
- Spices: ½ tsp salt
- 1 bay leaf
- 1 tsp dried thyme

Directions:

- Place eggplant in a large sieve and generously sprinkle with salt.
- Toss well and let it sit for 10-15 minutes.
- Grease the bottom of your pot with butter. Add onions and garlic. Cook for 3-4 minutes or until Now add the meat and briefly brown stirring constantly.
- Finally, pour in the beef broth and season with salt and thyme. Add bay leaves and give it a good stir.

- Seal the lid and set the steam release handle to the "Sealing" position.
- Press the "Meat" button.
- When you hear the end signal, perform a quick pressure release and open the lid.
- Serve immediately.

Nutrition:

- Calories - 498
- Fat - 26.1g
- Carbs - 4.3g
- Protein - 57g

HERBED CHICKEN SOUP

Serving: 2

Ingredients:

- ½ pound boneless, skinless chicken pieces, cubed
- 8 ounces kidney beans
- 2 cups chicken or vegetable broth
- ½ onion, chopped
- ½ red pepper, chopped
- ½ celery rib, chopped
- 1 tablespoon tomato paste
- 1 clove garlic, minced
- 1 teaspoon
- Herbes de Provence
- Salt and pepper to taste
- 1 ½ cups baby spinach
- 2 tablespoons Parmesan cheese

Directions:

- Combine all the ingredients EXCEPT the spinach and Parmesan in a slow cooker.
- Cover, and cook on LOW for 4-5 hours. The chicken should be tender and cooked through.
- Stir in the spinach, and cook for 30 minutes more, until wilted.
- Serve with a topping of Parmesan cheese.

Nutrition:

- Calories - 331
- Fat - 10 g
- Carbs - 27 g
- Protein - 33 g

CHILI VERDE

Serving: 6

Ingredients:

- For chili: 2 lbs beef stew meat
- 1 cup tomatillos, chopped
- 1 cup cherry tomatoes, chopped
- 1 onion, finely chopped
- 3 garlic cloves, crushed
- 2 Serrano peppers, chopped
- 3 cups beef broth
- 3 tbsp oil
- Spices: 1 tsp salt
- ½ tsp chili powder
- ¼ tsp freshly ground black pepper

Directions:

- Plug in the instant pot and press the "Saute" button. Grease the stainless steel insert with oil and add onions and garlic.
- Briefly cook for 3-4 minutes and add the remaining ingredients.
- Give it a good stir and seal the lid. Set the steam release handle to the "Sealing" position and press the "MANUAL" button.
- Set the timer for 20 minutes on high pressure.
- When done, release the pressure by moving the pressure valve to the "Venting" position.
- Carefully open the lid and stir well again making sure to break down the tomatillos.
- Optionally, sprinkle with some freshly chopped parsley or Parmesan cheese and serve immediately

Nutrition:

- Calories - 383
- Fat - 17.2g
- Carbs - 4g
- Protein - 49.1g

CHANAFLOWER MASALA

Serving: 4

Ingredients:

- 2 cups chopped raw cauliflower
- 1 can chopped tomatoes

- 1 cup water
- 1 onion, minced
- 4 tbsp. chana masala mix
- 1 tbsp. oil
- salt and pepper

Directions:

- Warm the oil in your Instant Pot.
- Soften the onion 5 minutes.
- Mix all the ingredients in your Instant Pot.
- Seal and cook on Stew for 10 minutes.
- Release the pressure quickly and stir well.
- Rest before serving.

Nutrition:

- Calories - 100
- Fat - 5.5g
- Carbs - 10g
- Protein - 2g

OSSO BUCO

Serving: 8

Ingredients:

- 3lbs oxtail
- 2 cups chopped onion
- 1 tin chopped tomatoes
- 1 cup chopped carrot
- 1 cup chopped celery
- ½ cup red wine

- 8 chopped garlic cloves
- ¼ ounce mushrooms
- 1 tbsp. oil, split in half
- salt and pepper
- parsley, lemon zest, bay leaf

Directions:

- Put the Instant Pot on high heat with half a tablespoon of oil and the onions.
- After five minutes, add the remaining oil and the beef.
- After turning the beef for 10 minutes to brown it a little, add the remaining ingredients.
- Cover with stock or water and cook on Stew for 45 minutes.

Nutrition:

- Calories - 186
- Fat - 6g
- Carbs - 9g
- Protein - 24g

CREAMY SPINACH SOUP

Serving: 2

Ingredients:

- For soup: 3 cups spinach, chopped
- 1 cup cauliflower, chopped
- 3 cups beef broth
- ½ cup heavy cream

- 2 tbsp butter
- Spices: ¼ tsp sea salt
- ½ tsp black pepper, freshly ground
- 1 tsp garlic powder

Directions:

- Plug in your instant pot and set the stainless steel insert.
- Place spinach in a large sieve and rinse well under running water. Stir well and pour in the broth. Seal the lid and set the steam release handle to the "Sealing" position. Press the "MANUAL" button and set the timer for 10 minutes on high pressure.
- When done, press the „Cancel"button and release the pressure naturally for 10-15
- minutes. Then move the pressure valve to the "Venting" position to release any remaining pressure.
- Carefully, open the lid and stir in two tablespoons of butter.
- Chill for a while.
- Serve immediately.

Nutrition:

- Calories - 286
- Fat - 24.9g
- Carbs - 4.3g
- Protein - 10.3g

INSTANT POT HAM AND POTATO SOUP

Serving: 5

Ingredients:

- 2 tablespoons butter
- 1 onion, diced
- 8 cloves of garlic, minced
- 2 pounds Yukon Gold potatoes, cut into small chunks
- 4 cups chicken broth
- A dash of cayenne pepper
- ½ cup cheddar cheese, grated
- 1 cup cooked ham, diced
- Salt and pepper
- 2 tablespoons fried bacon bits

Directions:

- Press the Saute button on the Instant Pot.
- Heat the butter and saute the onions and garlic until fragrant.
- Stir in the potatoes and cook for 3 minutes.
- Pour in the broth, cayenne pepper, cheese, and cooked ham. Season with salt and pepper to taste.
- Close the lid and press the Manual button.
- Adjust the cooking time to 25 minutes.
- Do quick pressure release.
- Open the lid and garnish with bacon bits on top.

Nutrition:

- Calories - 394
- Carbs - 46.7g
- Protein - 24.5g
- Fat - 13.3g

FISH AND SEAFOOD

TROUT WITH BROCCOLI

Serving: 5

Ingredients:

- 2 lbs. trout fillets, skin-on
- 2 tbsps. butter
- 2 tbsps. apple cider vinegar
- 4 cups fish stock
- 3 cups broccoli, chopped
- 1 small onion, finely chopped
- ¼ cup olive oil
- ½ tsp. chili flakes
- ¼ tsp. garlic powder
- ½ tsp. dried celery
- 1 tsp. chili powder
- ½ tsp. salt

Directions:

- Remove the fish from the refrigerator about an hour before using. Rub with olive oil and sprinkle with salt, dried celery, chili powder, chili flakes, and garlic powder. Place in a deep bowl and cover with a lid. Set aside.

- Plug in the Instant Pot and pour in the fish stock. Add broccoli and stir well. Seal the lid
- and set the steam release handle to the "Sealing" position. Set the timer for 20 minutes.
- When done, perform a quick pressure release and open the lid. Remove the cauliflower from the pot and drain. Place in a deep bowl and mash with a potato masher. Optionally, a
- food processor and process until smooth. Set aside.
- Place the steam insert in the pot and place the fish in it. Pour in 2 cups of water and seal the lid. Set the steam release handle again and press the "Fish" button.
- When done; perform a quick pressure release and open the lid. Remove the fish from the pot and press the "Saute" button.
- Add mashed broccoli and stir in the butter. Optionally, sprinkle with some salt and garlic powder. Heat up and remove from the pot. Serve with steamed fish.

Nutrition:

- Calories - 488
- Fat - 27.2g
- Protein - 54.2g
- Carbs - 3.3g
- Carbs - 1.6g
- Sugar - 0.0g

JAMAICAN FISH STEW

Serving: 4

Ingredients:

- ¼ cup butter
- 6 oz yellow onion
- 1 teaspoon minced garlic
- 1 red sweet pepper
- 1 cup tomatoes, chopped
- 5 oz coconut milk
- 1-pound cod fillet
- 1 teaspoon salt
- ½ teaspoon ground black pepper
- 1 tablespoon garlic sauce

Directions:

- Toss the butter into the slow cooker bowl. Add the minced garlic, chopped tomatoes, salt, ground black pepper, and garlic sauce.
- Slice the sweet red pepper and add it to the slow cooker. Add the coconut milk. Dice the yellow onion and add it in the slow cooker too.
- Close the lid and cook for 3 hours on HIGH or until the vegetables are soft.
- Chop the cod fillet roughly.
- Add the chopped cod after 3 hours of cooking and cook the stew for 45 minutes more on HIGH. Then stir the dish gently to not damage the fish and serve.
- Enjoy!

Nutrition:

- Calories - 336
- Fat - 25.4
- Carbs - 8.9
- Protein - 19

SHRIMP DIABLO

Serving: 4

Ingredients:

- 1 spaghetti squash (approximately 2 cups when cooked
- 1 cup onion, sliced
- 4 cloves garlic, crushed and minced
- 1 cup chicken or seafood stock
- 1 teaspoon salt
- 1 teaspoon black pepper
- 1 pound shrimp, cleaned and deveined
- ¼ cup butter, melted
- 1 tablespoon crushed red pepper flakes
- 1 teaspoon cayenne powder
- 1 teaspoon oregano
- 1 tablespoon lemon juice

Directions:

- Using a fork or sharp knife, poke 12-15 holes or small cuts in the surface of the spaghetti squash and place it in the center of the slow cooker.

- Add the onion, garlic, chicken stock, salt, and black pepper around the squash. Cover, and cook on low for 6 hours.
- Remove the spaghetti squash from the slow cooker and turn the heat to high.
- Allow the squash to cool just enough to handle before cutting it in half and scooping the insides back into the slow cooker. Discard the empty shell.
- Give the contents of the slow cooker a quick toss to mix the ingredients.
- Add the shrimp, melted butter, crushed red pepper flakes, cayenne powder, oregano, and lemon juice to the slow cooker.
- Cover and cook 10-15 minutes, or until the shrimp are cooked through.

Nutrition:

- Calories - 252.7
- Fat - 13.1 g
- Carbs - 8.7 g
- Protein - 25 g

TILAPIA PESTO

Serving: 4

Ingredients:

- 1 cup pesto
- 4 tilapia fillets
- ¼ cup tomato paste
- 1 cup onion, diced

- 1 teaspoon salt
- ½ teaspoon black pepper
- 1 medium lemon, sliced

Directions:

- You are going to cook these fillets in four separate foil packets, so lay a sheet (or four of aluminum foil on the countertop.
- Spread ¼ cup of pesto in the center of each sheet of foil.
- Place 1 fillet on top of each layer of pesto.
- Spread 1 tablespoon of tomato paste across each fillet.
- Place ¼ cup onion over the tomato paste.
- Salt and pepper each fillet to taste.
- Place a couple of slices of lemon over each fillet.
- Seal the foil packets by folding tightly. Now you can place the packets into freezer bags and freeze or cook immediately.
- If cooking now, cook on low for 2 hours.
- If cooking from frozen, cook on low for 4 hours.

Nutrition:

- Calories - 420
- Fat - 28 g
- Carbs - 9 g
- Protein - 32 g

BUTTERY SALMON WITH ONIONS AND CARROTS

Serving: 4

Ingredients:

- 4 salmon fillets
- 4 tablespoons butter
- 4 onions, chopped
- 16 ounces baby carrots
- 3 cloves garlic, minced
- Salt and pepper

Directions:

- Melt butter in the microwave, and pour into the slow cooker.
- Add onions, garlic, and baby carrots.
- Cover and cook for 6-7 hours on LOW, stirring occasionally until vegetables begin to caramelize.
- Place fillet over vegetables in slow cooker, and season with salt and pepper.
- Cover and cook on LOW for 1-2 hours until salmon flakes.
- Serve on a serving plate, and top with onion mixture.

Nutrition:

- Calories - 367
- Fat - 22 g
- Carbs - 12.2 g
- Protein - 39 g

SALMON CURRY

Serving: 4

Ingredients:

- 14 oz salmon fillet
- 1 cup of coconut milk
- 1 tablespoon curry paste
- 1/3 jalapeno pepper, chopped
- ½ teaspoon garlic powder
- 1 teaspoon coconut oil
- ½ white onion, sliced

Directions:

- Put sliced onion, coconut oil, garlic powder, chopped jalapeno pepper, and curry paste in the crockpot.
- Mix up the mixture well.
- After this, chop the salmon fillet roughly and Add coconut milk and close the lid.
- Cook the salmon curry for 1.5 hours on High.

Nutrition:

- Calories - 311
- Fat - 23.8
- Carbs - 6
- Protein - 21

TASTY CRAB LEGS

Serving: 4-6

Ingredients:

- 4 lbs king crab legs, broken in half
- 1 cup water
- ¼ cup butter
- 3 lemon wedges

Directions:

- Pour the water into the Instant Pot and insert a steamer basket.
- Place the crab legs on the rack.
- Close and lock the lid. Select MANUAL and cook at HIGH pressure for 3 minutes.
- When the timer goes off, use aQuick Release. Carefully open the lid.

SHRIMP SOUP

Serving: 6

Ingredients:

- ½ cup snap peas
- 12 oz shrimps, peeled
- 4 oz fennel bulb, chopped
- ½ teaspoon ground nutmeg
- ½ teaspoon salt
- 1 teaspoon coriander seeds
- 2 cups of water

- 2 cups of coconut milk
- 1 teaspoon chili powder
- ½ teaspoon smoked paprika
- 1 cup kale, chopped

Directions:

- Put fennel bulb, ground nutmeg, salt, coriander seeds, water, coconut milk, chili powder, and smoked paprika in the crockpot.
- Close the lid and cook the liquid on High for 2 hours.
- Then add chopped kale, snap peas, and shrimps.
- Close the lid and cook soup for 30 minutes on High.

Nutrition:

- Calories - 275
- Fat - 20.3
- Carbs - 10
- Protein - 16

SQUID STEW

Serving: 4

Ingredients:

- 17 ounces squid
- 1 and ½ tablespoons red chili powder
- Salt and black pepper to the taste
- ¼ teaspoon turmeric powder
- 2 cups veggie stock

- 4 garlic cloves, minced
- 1 teaspoon ginger powder
- ½ teaspoons cumin, ground
- 3 tablespoons olive oil
- ¼ teaspoon mustard seeds, toasted

Directions:

- Put squids in your slow cooker, add chili powder, salt, pepper, turmeric, stock, garlic, ginger, cumin, oil and mustard seeds, stir, cover and cook on High for 2 hours.
- Enjoy!

Nutrition:

- Calories - 241
- Fat - 1
- Carbs - 12
- Protein - 3

SHELLFISH JAMBALAYA

Serving: 4

Ingredients:

- 8 oz crushed tomatoes
- 14 oz diced tomatoes, undrained
- Juice and zest of 1/2 lemon
- 1 small yellow onion, chopped
- 2 celery ribs, sliced thinly
- 1 red or yellow or orange bell pepper, chopped
- 3 garlic cloves, chopped

- 1/2 bay leaf
- 1/2 tsp dried oregano
- 1/2 tsp sweet paprika
- 1/3 tsp sea salt
- 1/3 tsp dried thyme
- 1/4 tsp hot pepper sauce
- 1/4 tsp cayenne pepper
- 1/4 tsp freshly cracked black pepper
- 1/2 lb fresh bay scallops
- 1/2 lb fresh shrimp, shelled and deveined
- 1/4 cup chopped fresh parsley
- 1 1/2 cups cooked long grain brown rice
- Sucanat or xylithol

Directions:

- Stir together the onion, bell pepper, tomatoes, celery, lemon zest, paprika, thyme, oregano, hot sauce, salt, and pepper. Stir in a dash of Sucanat or xylithol, then add the bay leaf.
- Cover and cook for 3 hours on high or for 7 hours on low.
- Set heat to high, then stir in the scallops and shrimp. Cover and cook for 15 minutes, or until the shellfish are cooked through.
- Add the lemon juice, then stir in the parsley.
- Place the hot brown rice on a platter and ladle the jambalaya on top. Serve at once.

Nutrition:

- Calories - 237

SALMON PIE

Serving: 8

Ingredients:

- 10 oz yeast dough
- 1 teaspoon olive oil
- 1-pound salmon
- 1 tablespoon lemon juice
- ¼ cup cream cheese
- 6 oz Cheddar cheese shredded
- 1 tablespoon oregano
- 1 teaspoon salt
- 2 large eggs
- 1 cup onion, diced

Directions:

- Brush the parchment with the olive oil and put it in the slow cooker.
- Roll the dough and put it in the slow cooker too. Beat the eggs in the bowl and whisk. Combine the whisked eggs with the lemon juice, cream cheese, oregano, salt, and diced onion.
- Chop the salmon and add it to the whisked egg mixture.
- Then pour the fish mixture into the rolled dough. Cover the pie with the shredded cheese and close the lid. Cook the salmon pie for 9 hours on LOW.
- When the pie is cooked, it will have a golden brown surface. From the slow cooker and cut into pieces. Serve warm. Enjoy!

Nutrition:

- Calories - 237
- Fat - 10.1
- Carbs - 11
- Protein - 24

EASY SEAFOOD SOUP

Serving: 12

Ingredients:

- 10 ounces canned coconut cream
- 2 cups veggie stock
- 2 cups tomato sauce
- 1 cup Paleo shrimp cocktail sauce
- 12 ounces canned crab meat
- 1 and ½ cups water
- 1 pound small shrimp, peeled and deveined
- 1 pound jumbo shrimp, peeled and deveined
- 1 yellow onion, chopped
- 1 cup carrots, chopped
- 4 tilapia fillets, cubed
- 2 celery stalks, chopped
- 3 kale stalks, chopped
- 1 bay leaf
- 2 garlic cloves, minced
- A pinch of sea salt
- ½ teaspoon cloves, ground
- 1 teaspoon rosemary, dried
- 1 teaspoon thyme, dried

Directions:

- In your slow cooker, mix coconut cream with stock, tomato sauce, shrimp cocktail sauce and water and stir.
- Add small and jumbo shrimp, fish cubes, onion, carrots, celery, kale, garlic, bay leaf, salt, cloves, thyme and rosemary, stir, cover and cook on Low for 3 hours.
- Stir soup again, ladle into bowls and serve.
- Enjoy!

Nutrition:

- Calories - 220
- Fat - 3
- Carbs - 8
- Protein - 13

SPICY SHRIMP KETO PASTA

Serving: 4

Ingredients:

- 7 oz shrimps, cleaned
- 2 cups cauliflower, chopped into florets
- 2 garlic cloves, crushed
- 2 tbsp olive oil
- 1 tsp apple cider vinegar
- ¼ cup mayonnaise
- 1 cup cream cheese
- 3 cups chicken stock
- Spices: 1 tsp smoked salt

- ½ tsp onion powder
- ½ tsp red pepper flakes

Directions:

- Place shrimps and cauliflower in the pot. Add garlic and pour in the stock. Sprinkle with olive oil and apple cider and stir well.
- Seal the lid and set the steam release handle to the "Sealing" position. Press the "MANUAL" button and cook for 9 minutes on high pressure.
- When done, perform a quick release and open the lid. Remove the shrimp mixture and drain the remaining liquid in the pot.
- Now press the "Saute" button and heat up the inner pot. add cream cheese and mayonnaise. Season with smoked salt, onion powder, and red pepper flakes.
- Briefly cook, for about a minute and stir in the shrimp mixture.
- Mix well and press the "Cancel" button.
- Serve immediately and optionally sprinkle with some shredded mozzarella or grated parmesan.

Nutrition:

- Calories - 401
- Fat - 33.5g
- Carbs - 8.2g
- Protein - 17.4g

SEAFOOD PAELLA

Serving: 6

Ingredients:

- 2 cups chopped white fish and scallops
- 2 cups mussels and shrimp
- 4 tbsp olive oil
- 1 onion, diced
- 1 red bell pepper, diced
- 1 green bell pepper, diced
- 2 cups rice
- A few saffron threads
- 2 cups fish stock
- Salt and ground black pepper to taste

Directions:

- Set your instant pot on SAUTe mode, add the oil and heat it up.
- Add the onion and bell peppers and saute for 4 minutes.
- Add the fish, rice, and saffron, stir. Cook for 2 minutes more.
- Pour in the fish stock and season with salt and pepper, stir.
- Place the shellfish on top.
- Press the CANCEL key to stop the SAUTe function.
- Close and lock the lid. Select MANUAL and cook at HIGH pressure for 6 minutes.
- Once cooking is complete, select CANCEL and let

- Naturally Release
- for 10 minutes. Release any remaining steam manually. Uncover the pot.
- Stir the dish and let sit for 5 minutes. Serve.

SHRIMP FISH CURRY MEAL

Serving: 6

Ingredients:

- 1 (14.5 ounce can diced tomatoes
- 1 (13 ounce) can full-fat coconut milk
- 1 pound shrimp
- 1 pound tilapia fillets, chopped into bite-sized pieces
- Juice of 1 lime
- 1 tablespoon olive oil
- 2 green onions, chopped
- 1 red bell pepper, chopped
- 2 cups peas, cut into slices
- ½ cup cilantro, chopped
- 1 teaspoon red pepper flakes
- 1 teaspoon salt
- 1 teaspoon black pepper (ground)

Directions:

- Take your Instant Pot and open the top lid.
- Press "SAUTE" mode.
- Add the oil and heat it; stir-cook the fish and shrimp until tender.
- Add remaining ingredients except for the milk; gently stir.

- Close the top lid and seal the pressure valve.
- Press "MANUAL" setting with 3 minutes of cooking time and "HIGH" pressure mode.
- Press "QPR" function to release the pressure.
- Open the lid; mix in the milk, Enjoy!

Nutrition:

- Calories - 106
- Fat - 2g
- Carbs - 9g
- Sodium - 264mg
- Protein - 6g

CLASSIC LOBSTER TOMATO STEW

Serving: 4

Ingredients:

- 4 lobster tails, defrosted
- 2 cups cherry tomatoes, chopped
- 2 cups fish stock
- 1 cup celery, finely chopped
- 2 shallots, diced
- 2 cups heavy cream
- 3 tbsp olive oil
- 2 tbsp butter
- Spices: 1 tbsp Old Bay seasoning
- 1 tsp dill
- 1 tsp black pepper, freshly ground
- ½ tsp smoked paprika

Directions:

- In a large bowl, combine tomatoes, celery, shallots, olive oil, and dill.
- Mix until well incorporated and set aside.
- Plug in the instant pot and press the "Saute" button. Grease the inner pot with butter and add lobster tails. Season with salt, pepper, and Old Bay seasoning. Cook for 3-4 minutes on each side.
- Pour in the tomato mixture, fish stock, and sprinkle with smoked paprika.
- Give it a good stir and seal the lid. Set the steam release handle and press the "MANUAL" button.
- Set the timer for 5 minutes on high pressure.
- When done, press the "Cancel" button and release the pressure naturally. Carefully open the lid and stir in the heavy cream.
- Chill for a while and serve.

Nutrition:

- Calories - 468
- Fat - 40.3g
- Carbs - 5.3g
- Protein - 21.2g

SCALLOPS WITH CHERRY SAUCE

Serving: 4

Ingredients:

- 1-pound scallops
- 1 teaspoon salt
- 1 teaspoon ground white pepper
- ½ teaspoon olive oil
- 2 tablespoons lemon juice
- 1 cup cherry, pitted
- 1 tablespoon cornstarch
- 3 tablespoons sugar
- ½ teaspoon ground ginger
- 1 tablespoon flour

Directions:

- Sprinkle the scallops with the salt, ground white pepper, and lemon juice.
- Spray the slow cooker bowl with the olive oil and put the scallops inside the bowl. Close the lid and cook the seafood for 30 minutes on HIGH.
- Meanwhile, put the cherries in a blender and blend them until smooth. Then Combine the cornstarch and flour together then add the dry ingredients into the slow cooker bowl and mix with a hand blender.
- Stir the sauce until it starts to thicken.
- Add the ground ginger and stir it carefully.
- When the time is over, open the slow cooker lid and sprinkle the scallops with the cherry sauce.

Stir gently and cook the dish on LOW for 2 minutes more.
- Serve the dish immediately. Enjoy!

Nutrition:

- Calories - 150
- Fat - 1.3
- Carbs - 20.11
- Protein - 15

SHRIMP ZOODLES MEAL

Serving: 4

Ingredients:

- 1 cup veggie stock
- 2 tablespoons olive oil
- 3 teaspoons minced garlic
- 4 cups zucchini noodles
- 2 tablespoon ghee
- Juice of ½ lemon
- 1 tablespoon chopped basil
- 1-pound shrimp, peeled and deveined
- ½ teaspoon paprika

Directions:

- Take your Instant Pot; open the top lid. Plug it and turn it on.
- Press "SAUTe" setting and the pot will start heating up.

- In the cooking pot area, add the oil, ghee, and garlic.
- Cook for 1 minute and add the shrimp and lemon juice.
- Cook for 1 more minute. Add the zoodles, paprika, and stock.
- Close the top lid and seal its valve.
- Press "MANUAL" setting. Adjust cooking time to 3 minutes.
- Allow the recipe to cook for the set cooking time.
- After the set cooking time ends, press "CANCEL" and then press "QPR (Quick Pressure Release".
- Instant Pot will quickly release the pressure.
- Open the top lid, add the cooked recipe mix in serving plates. Top with basil.
- Serve and enjoy!

Nutrition:

- Calories - 287
- Fat - 19.5g
- Carbs - 5g
- Protein - 29g

SALMON POTATOES RECIPE

Serving: 6

Ingredients:

- 4 to 5 medium potatoes, peeled, sliced
- 3 tablespoons flour
- Salt and pepper, to taste

- 1 can (16 ounces salmon, drained, flaked
- ½ cup onion, chopped
- 1 can (10¾ ounces) cream of mushroom or celery soup
- ¼ cup water
- Dash nutmeg
- (optional)

Directions:

- Place the ingredients into the slow cooker, by layer, in this order, twice: - ½ of the potatoes
- - ½ of the flour
- - salt and pepper
- - ½ of the salmon
- - ½ of the onion
- - Soup
- - Nutmeg
- (optional)
- Cook everything on LOW for 7 to 9 hours.

Nutrition:

- Calories - 335
- Fat - 16 g
- Carbs - 41 g
- Protein - 14 g

INSTANT POT LOBSTER ROLL

Serving: 6

Ingredients:

- 1 ½ cups chicken broth
- 1 teaspoon old bay seasoning
- 2 pounds lobster tails, raw and in the shell
- 1 lemon, halved
- 3 scallions, chopped
- ½ cup mayonnaise
- 4 tablespoons unsalted butter
- ¼ teaspoon celery salt

Directions:

- Pour the broth into the Instant Pot and sprinkle with old bay seasoning.
- Place a steamer on top and lay each lobster tail shell side down.
- Squeeze the first half of the lemon over the lobsters.
- Close the lid and press the Manual button.
- Adjust the cooking time to 6 minutes.
- While cooking, prepare the sauce by combining the rest of the ingredients in a bowl.
- Once the timer beeps off, do quick pressure release.
- Brush the mayo dip on the exposed meat of the lobster tails.

Nutrition:

- Calories - 392
- Carbs - 2.7g
- Protein - 47.5g
- Fat - 20.2g

CHICKEN AND POULTRY

TURKEY CASSEROLE

Serving: 6

Ingredients:

- 2 lbs boneless turkey breast, about 4 pieces
- 1 medium-sized onion, sliced
- 1 celery stalk, sliced
- 1 bag (10 oz frozen mixed vegetables
- ½ tsp salt
- ½ tsp ground black pepper
- 1 cup chicken broth
- 2 small cans of creamy mushroom soup
- 1 bag (14 oz) Pepperidge Farm herb stuffing mix

Directions:

- Add the onion, celery, and frozen mixed vegetables to the Instant Pot.
- Season the turkey breast with salt and pepper.
- Add the breasts to the pot. Pour the broth into the pot. Close and lock the lid.
- Select the POULTRY setting and set the cooking time for 25 minutes.
- When the timer goes off, use aQuick Release. Carefully open the lid.

- Pour the mushroom soup into the pot and add stuffing mix.
- Select the SAUTe setting and cook for another 8 minutes, stirring occasionally.

CREAMY GARLIC MUSHROOM CHICKEN STEW

Serving: 4

Ingredients:

- 1 brown onion; sliced.
- 7 -ounce mix of Swiss brown and white button mushrooms
- 4 large garlic cloves; diced.
- 2 tablespoon olive oil
- 1 teaspoon salt
- 1.7-pound chicken thighs or breast; diced.
- 1-2 bay leaves
- 1/4 teaspoon nutmeg powder
- 1/2 teaspoon black pepper
- 1/2 cup chicken stock
- 1 teaspoon Dijon mustard
- 1/3 cup sour cream
- 1 teaspoon arrowroot; cornstarch, or tapioca starch for thickening
- 2-3 tablespoon parsley; chopped.

Directions:

- Turn the Instant Pot on and press the "SAUTE" function key.

- Combine the onion, olive oil, and salt in the pot. Cook for 3-4 minutes, until soft.
- Add the next eight ingredients and stir thoroughly.
- Press "KEEP WARM/CANCEL" * Put on and lock the lid, the steam releasing handle should point to Sealing
- Press "POULTRY" (High Pressure) for 15 minutes. After 3 beeps the pressure cooker will start. Let the pressure release naturally for 5 minutes, then use the quick release
- to let off the rest of the steam.
- Uncover and press the "SAUTE" function key again. Scoop out a few tablespoons of the liquid and dissolve in the arrowroot in it. Pour the mixture back into the pot and stir
- Stir in the sour cream. Press "KEEP WARM/CANCEL" to stop the cooking process
- Top with chopped parsley and serve.

Nutrition:

- Calories - 189
- Carbs - 5.6 g
- Carbs - 3 g
- Fat - 17 g
- Protein - 18 g

LIME AND SALSA CHICKEN WITH CAULIFLOWER RICE

Serving: 4

Ingredients:

- 2 Chicken Breasts
- ¼ cup Lime Juice
- ½ cup Mexican Cheese Blend
- ½ tsp Garlic Powder
- 3 tbsp. Olive Oil
- ½ cup Tomato Sauce
- ½ cup Salsa
- 2 cups riced Cauliflower
- Salt and Pepper, to taste

Directions:

- Combine all of the ingredients, except the cauliflower and cheese, in your IP.
- Close the lid and set the MANUAL cooking mode.
- Cook on HIGH for 12 minutes.
- Do a quick pressure release and add stir in the rice and cheese.
- Cook for 5 more minutes.
- Do a quick pressure release.
- Serve and enjoy!

Nutrition:

- Calories - 280
- Fat - 16g

- Carbs - 5g
- Protein - 19g

SWEET POTATO TURKEY MEAL

Serving: 4

Ingredients:

- 4 tablespoons dairy-free buffalo sauce
- 1 onion, diced
- 3 tablespoons ghee
- ½ teaspoon garlic powder
- 1 ½ pounds turkey breast, cut into cubes
- 1 pound sweet potatoes, cut into cubes

Directions:

- Switch on your instant pot after placing it on a clean and dry kitchen platform. Press "Saute" cooking function.
- Open the pot lid; add the 1 tablespoon ghee and onions in the pot; start cooking for 2-3 minutes to cook well and soften.
- Stir in the remaining ingredients.
- Close the pot by closing the top lid. Also, ensure to seal the valve.
- Press "Poultry" cooking function and set cooking time to 18 minutes. It will start cooking after a few minutes. Let the pot mix cook under pressure until the timer
- reads zero.
- Turn off and press "Cancel" cooking function. Quick release pressure.

- Open the pot and serve on a serving plate or bowl. Enjoy the Paleo dish!

Nutrition:

- Calories - 374
- Fat - 12.5g
- Carbs - 32g
- Protein - 36.5g

CHICKEN WITH MUSHROOMS AND MUSTARD

Serving: 4

Ingredients:

- 4 chicken breasts, halved
- 2 tablespoons flour
- 2 tablespoon vegetable oil
- 1 tablespoon butter
- 1 onion, chopped
- 1 cup mushrooms, sliced
- ½ cup light cream
- 1 tablespoon fresh parsley, chopped
- 1 tablespoon Dijon mustard
- 1 tablespoon lemon juice, freshly squeezed
- Salt and pepper

Directions:

- Pound the chicken breasts and dredge in the flour. Set aside.
- Press the Saute button on the Instant Pot.

- Heat the oil and butter and add the dredged chicken pieces. Cook on all sides for 3 minutes each.
- Add the rest of the ingredients.
- Close the lid and press the Poultry button.
- Adjust the cooking time to 10 minutes.
- Do quick pressure release.

Nutrition:

- Calories - 675
- Carbs - 8.4g
- Protein - 62.4g
- Fat - 42.6g

SHREDDED CHICKEN WITH SHIITAKE

Serving: 5

Ingredients:

- 6 shiitake mushrooms
- 1 lb chicken breast, boneless and skinless
- 1 ½ cup chicken stock
- 1 spring onion, finely chopped
- 4 tbsp sesame oil
- 2 tbsp butter
- 2 tbsp dark soy sauce
- 1 tbsp light soy sauce
- ½ tsp stevia powder
- 2 tsp rice vinegar
- Spices: 1 tbsp fresh ginger, grated
- ½ tsp pepper, freshly ground

- ½ tsp chili flakes

Directions:

- In a small bowl, whisk together oil, dark soy sauce, light soy sauce, stevia powder, rice vinegar, ginger, chili flakes, and pepper.
- Optionally, add some salt and set aside.
- Rinse the meat and place on a cutting board. Chop into smaller pieces and place at the bottom of your instant pot.
- Add spring onions and pour in the stock.
- Seal the lid and set the steam release handle to the "Sealing" position.
- Press the "Poultry" button and cook for 10 minutes.
- When you hear the cooker's end signal, perform a quick pressure release and open the lid. Remove the chicken from the pot and place in a deep bowl. Drizzle with the prepared soy mixture and shred with two forks.
- Set aside.
- Remove the remaining stock from the pot and press the "Saute" button.
- Grease the inner pot with butter and heat up.
- Add shiitake and briefly cook - for 3-4 minutes, stirring constantly.
- Now add the meat and give it a good stir.
- Cook for another 5 minutes.
- When done, remove from the pot and serve immediately.

Nutrition:

- Calories - 299
- Fat - 18.1g
- Carbs - 11.3g
- Protein - 21.7g

CHICKEN AND PINEAPPLE

Serving: 8

Ingredients:

- 6 boneless, skinless chicken breasts
- 30 oz canned pineapple chunks, not drained
- 3 Tbsp low sodium soy sauce or coconut aminos
- 2 cloves garlic, minced
- 12 oz canned sliced water chestnuts, drained
- 1 1/2 tsp grated fresh ginger
- 2 red bell peppers, chopped
- 1/2 cup honey or liquid noncaloric sweetener
- 1 1/2 Tbsp cornstarch

Directions:

- Combine the pineapple juice, garlic, honey or sweetener, soy sauce, ginger, and cornstarch in a bowl.
- Put the pineapples, water chestnuts, and chicken breasts into the slow cooker, then pour the pineapple juice mixture all over and turn to coat.
- Cover and cook for 6 hours on low.
- Remove the lid, stir in the bell peppers, and cook for an additional half hour.

- Best served with wild or brown rice (not included in the calorie count.

Nutrition:

- Calories - 255

OREGANO PASTA CHICKEN

Serving: 2

Ingredients:

- ½ teaspoon olive oil
- ½ cup diced tomatoes
- ½ cup diced red bell pepper
- ½ teaspoon oregano
- 1 bay leaf
- ½ cup chopped onion
- 1 ½ cup diced chicken
- ¼ teaspoon salt
- ½ teaspoon pepper
- 2 tablespoons chopped parsley
- Cooked pasta of your choice

Directions:

- Switch on the pot after placing it on a clean and dry platform. Press "Saute" cooking function.
- Open the pot lid; add the oil and onions in the pot; cook for 2 minutes to cook well and soften.
- Add the chicken, bell pepper, and diced tomatoes. Mix the salt, pepper, oregano, and bay leaf.

- Close the pot by closing the top lid. Also, ensure to seal the valve.
- Press "MANUAL" cooking function and set cooking time to 10 minutes. It
- will start cooking after a few minutes. Let the pot mix cook under pressure until the timer reads zero.
- Press "Cancel" cooking function and press "Natural release (NPR" setting. It will take 8-10 minutes for natural pressure release.
- Open the pot; top with some parsley and serve with cooked pasta!

Nutrition:

- Calories - 102
- Fat - 2.5g
- Carbs - 4g
- Protein - 15.5g

LEMONGRASS AND COCONUT CHICKEN

Serving: 4

Ingredients:

- 10 chicken drumsticks
- 1 onion, sliced
- 4 cloves of garlic, minced
- 1 stalk lemongrass, trimmed and cut to 2 inches thick
- 1 thumb-size ginger
- 2 tablespoons fish sauce

- 3 tablespoons soy sauce
- 1 teaspoon five spice powder
- 1 cup coconut milk
- ¼ cup cilantro, chopped
- Salt and pepper

Directions:

- Press the Saute button on the Instant Pot.
- Place the chicken, onion, and garlic. Cook until the chicken has rendered some oil and turn slightly brown. Cook for 6 minutes.
- Add the rest of the ingredients.
- Close the lid and press the Poultry button.
- Adjust the cooking time to 15 minutes.
- Do natural pressure release.

Nutrition:

- Calories - 711
- Carbs - 9.8 g
- Protein - 61.9g
- Fat - 46.3g

CHICKEN LEGS THE HUNGARIAN WAY

Serving: 4

Ingredients:

- 1 tbsp. Olive Oil
- ½ cup Sour Cream
- ½ cup Chicken Stock

- ½ Onion, diced
- 2 tsp Hot Paprika
- 1 Tomato, chopped
- 4 Chicken Legs
- Salt and Pepper, to taste

Directions:

- Heat the oil in your IP and add the chicken to it.
- Cook until golden on all sides.
- Add onions to the pot and saute for a few minutes, until soft.
- Stir in the hot paprika and chicken stock.
- Return the chicken to the pot and place the tomatoes on top.
- Close the lid and cook on MANUAL for 10 minutes.
- Press CANCEL and release the pressure.
- Season with salt and pepper, to taste.
- Pour the sauce over the chicken and serve.
- Enjoy!

Nutrition:

- Calories - 420
- Fat - 10g
- Carbs - 6g
- Protein - 30g

CHICKEN POT PIE

Serving: 8

Ingredients:

- 8 oz biscuit dough
- 1 cup sweet corn, frozen
- 1 cup green peas
- 11 oz chicken fillets
- 1 cup white onion, chopped
- 8 oz chicken creamy soup, canned
- 1 carrot
- 1 teaspoon onion powder
- 1 tablespoon ground paprika
- 1 teaspoon cilantro
- ½ teaspoon oregano
- 1 teaspoon turmeric
- 1 tablespoon salt
- 1 teaspoon butter
- 1 cup water

Directions:

- Chop the chicken fillets and put in the slow cooker. Sprinkle the chicken with the onion powder, ground paprika, cilantro, oregano, and turmeric.
- Add salt and green peas. Sprinkle the dish with the sweet corn. Peel the carrot and chop it. Add the chopped carrot and white onion to the slow cooker vessel.
- Then pour the water and chicken creamy soup in as well.

- Add butter and close the lid. Cook the dish on HIGH for 5 hours. Stir the mixture carefully. Cover the with the biscuit dough and close the lid.
- Cook the dish on HIGH for 3 hours more. Serve the prepared chicken pot pie immediately.
- Enjoy!

Nutrition:

- Calories - 283
- Fat - 10.9
- Carbs - 38.42
- Protein - 10

BALSAMIC CHICKEN WITH APPLE

Serving: 2

Ingredients:

- 4 chicken thighs, bone in, skinless
- ¼ teaspoon salt
- ½ teaspoon garlic powder
- ½ teaspoon rosemary, dried
- ¼ teaspoon paprika
- ¼ teaspoon pepper
- ¼ cup chicken broth
- ¼ cup apple juice
- 2 tablespoons balsamic vinegar
- 1 tablespoon lemon juice
- 1 tablespoon butter
- 1 tablespoon flour (gluten free, if needed

Directions:

- Arrange the chicken pieces in a 3-quart slow cooker, and sprinkle the seasonings over it.
- In a small mixing bowl, combine the broth, juice, vinegar, and lemon juice. Mix well, and pour the mixture over the chicken.
- Cover, and cook for 4-5 hours on LOW or until the chicken is tender and cooked through.
- When the chicken is done, remove it from the slow cooker and keep it warm.
- Melt the butter in a saucepan and add the flour. Stir until smooth.
- Now, slowly add the cooking liquid to the saucepan, and bring it to a boil. Stir until thickened, and serve it over the chicken.

Nutrition:

- Calories - 277
- Fat - 15 g
- Carbs - 9 g
- Protein - 25 g

TAIWANESE THREE CUP CHICKEN

Serving: 6

Ingredients:

- 2 tablespoon ginger; sliced into matchsticks
- 2-pound chicken thighs; boneless, skinless, cut in half.

- 6 dried red chilis
- 1/4 cup sesame oil
- 1/4 cup smashed garlic cloves
- 1/4 cup soy sauce
- 1/4 cup rice wine or pale dry sherry
- Salt; to taste
- 1/4 cup Thai basil; chopped
- 1/2 teaspoon xantham gum

Directions:

- Set Instant Pot to "SAUTE" . * Once hot, add the oil.
- Once the oil is hot, mix in the chilies, ginger, and garlic, and let them fry for 2 minutes until starting to crisp
- Add in the remaining ingredients, except for the basil.
- Cook for 7-10 minutes, then Natural Pressure Release
- Uncover and turn the pot on to "SAUTE" . *
- Add chopped basil leaves and stir.
- Once the liquid boils, sprinkle the xanthan gum and let it thicken. Serve hot.

Nutrition:

- Calories - 307
- Carbs - 7 g
- Carbs - 3.2 g
- Fat - 15 g
- Protein - 31g

STUFFED CHICKEN WITH TOMATOES

Serving: 8

Ingredients:

- 1 tablespoon honey
- 1 teaspoon turmeric
- 1 teaspoon coriander
- 1 teaspoon paprika
- 1 teaspoon cilantro
- 6 oz dried tomatoes
- 4 tablespoons fresh parsley
- 1 tablespoon mayonnaise
- 1 tablespoon ketchup
- 1 tablespoon butter
- 1 teaspoon salt
- 1 teaspoon ground black pepper
- 3-pounds chicken breast, skinless, boneless

Directions:

- Combine honey, turmeric, coriander, paprika, cilantro, salt, ground black pepper, and butter together. After this, combine the mayonnaise and ketchup together and whisk.
- Make the crosswise cut in the chicken breast. Rub with the melted butter mixture. Then rub with the mayonnaise mixture. Chop the dried tomatoes and fresh parsley.
- Fill the prepared chicken breast with the chopped dried tomatoes and parsley.

- Wrap the chicken breast in the foil and put in the slow cooker.
- Close the lid and cook on LOW for 10 hours. When the chicken is cooked, unwrap from the foil and slice then serve.

Nutrition:

- Calories - 330
- Fat - 17.9
- Carbs - 4.54
- Protein - 36

KETO DUCK BREAST WITH PROSCIUTTO

Serving: 4

Ingredients:

- 1-pound duck breasts
- 1 cup cremini mushrooms
- 2 tablespoon fresh parsley; finely chopped.
- 3 tablespoon apple cider vinegar
- 1 tablespoon orange zest
- 2 garlic cloves; crushed
- 1 shallot; finely chopped
- 1/2 cup duck fat
- 4 cups chicken broth
- 7-ounce prosciutto; chopped
- 1 teaspoon sea salt
- 1/2 teaspoon white pepper; freshly ground.

Directions:

- Plug in the instant pot and press the "SAUTE" button. Add duck fat and slowly melt, stirring constantly
- Now add shallots and garlic. Give it a good stir and cook for 2-3 minutes. Add mushrooms and continue to cook until the liquid has evaporated.
- Finally, add prosciutto and stir well. Briefly brown on all sides and press the "CANCEL" button.
- Add the meat in the pot and pour in the broth. Sprinkle with spices and orange zest. Pour in the cider and seal the lid
- Set the steam release handle to the "SEALING" position and press the "MANUAL" button.
- Set the timer for 20 minutes on high pressure
- When done, release the pressure naturally and carefully open the lid. Sprinkle with parsley and let it sit covered for about 10 minutes before serving

Nutrition:

- Calories - 496
- Fat - 34.3g
- Carbs - 3.5g
- Protein - 40.9g

SAVORY CHICKEN

Serving: 4

Ingredients:

- 2 red bell peppers, chopped
- 2 pounds chicken breasts, skinless and boneless
- 4 garlic cloves, minced
- 1 yellow onion, chopped
- 2 teaspoons paprika
- 1 cup low sodium chicken stock
- 2 teaspoons cinnamon powder
- ¼ teaspoon nutmeg, ground

Directions:

- In a bowl, mix bell peppers with chicken breasts, garlic, onion, paprika, cinnamon and nutmeg and toss to coat.
- Divide chicken and veggies between plates and serve.
- Enjoy!

Nutrition:

- Calories - 150
- Fat - 3
- Carbs - 7
- Protein - 10

QUICK AND EASY CHICKEN BROCCOLI CASSEROLE

Serving: 6

Ingredients:

- 5 boneless chicken breasts
- 1 can cream of broccoli with cheese soup
- ½ cup chicken broth
- 1 6-ounce package of stuffing for chicken, such as Stove Top
- 1 10-ounce bag frozen, chopped broccoli, thawed
- Cooking spray
- Salt and pepper

Directions:

- Spray slow cooker with cooking spray.
- Place chicken in the bottom of the slow cooker. Season with salt and pepper.
- Mix all remaining ingredients in a bowl, and pour on top of chicken.
- Cover and cook on LOW for 6-7 hours.

Nutrition:

- Calories - 280
- Fat - 13 g
- Carbs - 18.7 g
- Protein - 45.4 g

SPICED TURKEY

Serving: 4

Ingredients:

- 2 lbs. turkey breast, boneless
- 2 garlic cloves, crushed
- ¼ cup oil
- 3 cups chicken broth
- Spices: 1 tsp dried basil
- 3 whole cloves
- ½ tsp stevia powder

Directions:

- Rinse the meat under cold running water and pat dry with a kitchen towel. Place in a large Ziploc bag and add basil, cloves, and oil. Pour in one cup of chicken broth and seal the bag.
- Shake well and refrigerate for 20 minutes.
- Grease the stainless steel insert with some oil and add garlic. Stir-fry for 2 minutes. Remove the turkey from the refrigerator and place in the pot along with 2 tablespoons of the marinade and the remaining chicken broth.
- Seal the lid and set the steam release handle. Press the "MANUAL" button and set the timer for 25 minutes.
- When done, release the pressure naturally.

Nutrition:

- Calories - 313
- Fat - 20.3g
- Carbs - 8.7g
- Protein - 20.3g

CHICKEN FAJITAS

Serving: 4

Ingredients:

- 1 lb chicken breast, chopped into bite-sized pieces
- 2 tbsp homemade taco seasoning
- 1 cup cherry tomatoes, chopped
- 3 garlic cloves, minced
- 1 bell pepper, cut into strips
- 1 onion, finely chopped
- 1 tbsp lime juice
- 6 large leaves Iceberg lettuce
- For homemade taco seasoning: 3 tbsp chili powder
- 1 tsp onion powder
- 2 tbsp pink Himalayan salt
- 2 tsp garlic powder
- 2 tsp oregano
- 1 tbsp smoked paprika
- ½ tsp coriander powder
- ½ tsp black pepper, freshly ground

Directions:

- Combine all ingredients for taco seasoning in a jar and shake well.
- Set aside.
- Rinse well the meat and place in a deep bowl. Generously sprinkle with taco seasoning. Place in the pot and add tomatoes, garlic, sliced peppers, onions, and lime juice.
- Seal the lid and press the "Poultry" button. Set the timer for 8 minutes on high pressure.
- When done, perform a quick release and open the lid. Remove the mixture from the pot and place in a bowl.
- Cool completely.
- Spread about 2-3 tablespoons of the mixture at the center of each lettuce leaf and wrap tightly.
- Secure each wrap with a toothpick and serve immediately.

Nutrition:

- Calories - 322
- Fat - 6.1g
- Carbs - 11.4g
- Protein - 50.4g

INDIAN CHICKEN DISH

Serving: 6

Ingredients:

- 2 cups tomato puree
- ½ cup cashews, chopped, soaked for a couple of hours and drained

- ¼ cup water
- 2 and ½ pounds chicken thighs, skinless, boneless and cubed
- 2 and ½ tablespoons garam masala
- 2 garlic cloves, minced
- ½ yellow onion, chopped
- 1 teaspoon ginger powder
- A pinch of sea salt
- A pinch of cayenne pepper
- ½ teaspoon sweet paprika
- ½ cup cilantro, chopped

Directions:

- Put the tomato puree in your slow cooker.
- Add chicken pieces, garlic, garam masala, onion, ginger powder, a pinch of salt, cayenne pepper and paprika.
- Stir, cover and cook on Low for 6 hours.
- Meanwhile, in your blender, mix cashews with the water and pulse really well.
- Add this to your chicken, stir well, divide into bowls and sprinkle cilantro on top.
- Enjoy!

Nutrition:

- Calories - 189
- Fat - 3
- Carbs - 7
- Protein - 14

RUSTIC ITALIAN CHICKEN

Serving: 6

Ingredients:

- 1 ½ pounds bone-in chicken pieces
- 1 tablespoon olive oil
- 1 teaspoon black pepper
- 4 cloves garlic, sliced
- 1 cup tomatoes, chopped
- 2 cups green beans, trimmed
- 1 tablespoon anchovy paste
- ¼ cup Worcestershire sauce
- ¼ cup red wine
- ½ cup water
- ½ cup goat cheese

Directions:

- Drizzle the chicken with the olive oil, and season it with salt and black pepper. Place the chicken in the slow cooker.
- Add the garlic, tomatoes, and green beans.
- In a small bowl, combine the anchovy paste, Worcestershire sauce, red wine, and water.
- Pour the liquid into the slow cooker, cover, and cook on low for 8 hours.
- A few minutes before serving, remove the lid and sprinkle the dish with goat cheese.
- Cover and continue cooking just long enough for the goat cheese to become lightly melted before serving.

Nutrition:

- Calories - 220.8
- Fat - 8 g
- Carbs - 5.4 g
- Protein - 29 g

TURKEY MINESTRONE

Serving: 8

Ingredients:

- 7 oz chicken thighs
- 1-pound turkey breast
- 7 cup water
- 6 oz diced tomatoes
- 1 teaspoon kosher salt
- 1 teaspoon ground black pepper
- ½ teaspoon paprika
- 1 teaspoon cilantro
- ½ teaspoon ground cu minutes
- 1 tablespoon garlic clove
- 1 oz bay leaf
- 6 oz pasta, cooked
- 3 oz Swiss chard
- 2 zucchinis
- 1/3 cup red kidney beans, cooked

Directions:

- Put the chicken thighs and turkey breast in the slow cooker bowl. Add the water and diced onions. After this, add the kosher salt, ground black pepper, paprika, and cilantro.

- Then add the ground cumin and garlic cloves.
- Sprinkle the mixture with the bay leaf and cook on HIGH for 5 hours. When the time is done, remove the poultry from the slow cooker and shred well.
- Chop the zucchini and Swiss chard.
- Add the vegetables in the slow cooker. Then add the red kidney beans and shredded chicken and turkey. Close the lid and cook the dish for 3 hours on LOW.
- After this, add the cooked pasta and stir it carefully. Ladle the soup into the serving bowls and enjoy!

Nutrition:

- Calories - 173
- Fat - 6.6
- Carbs - 10.79
- Protein - 18

CROCK POT CHICKEN TIKKA MASALA

Serving: 6

Ingredients:

- 3 pounds chicken, cut into 1-inch cubes
- 1 cup tomatoes, diced
- 6 ounces chicken breast, cut into 1-inch pieces
- 2 tablespoons olive oil

- 1 onion, chopped
- 3 garlic cloves, minced
- 1 teaspoon ground ginger
- 3 tablespoons tomato paste
- 2 teaspoons smoked paprika
- 1 teaspoon cumin powder
- ¼ cup garam masala
- 1 cup heavy cream
- 1 cup coconut milk
- 1 teaspoon salt
- Fresh coriander for topping

Directions:

- Add the oil, chicken and all the dry spices to the crock pot.
- Add the diced tomatoes, onion, ginger, garlic, tomato paste, salt and coconut milk. Mix together thoroughly.
- Cook on low for 6 hours or high for 3 hours.
- Once the chicken is done, add in the heavy cream and mix.
- Garnish with some fresh coriander and cream.

Nutrition:

- Calories - 219
- Fat - 20 g
- Carbs - 5 g
- Protein - 41 g

GARLIC SPICED TURKEY

Serving: 2-3

Ingredients:

- 14-ounce turkey fillet, roughly chopped
- 1 teaspoon chili pepper
- 1 teaspoon (ground black pepper
- 3 tablespoons chicken stock
- 1 garlic clove, chopped
- 1 teaspoon ghee
- 1 tomato, chopped
- 1 teaspoon olive oil
- 1 teaspoon cilantro
- ½ teaspoon chopped parsley

Directions:

- Combine the chili pepper, (ground) black pepper, chopped tomato, olive oil, cilantro, chopped parsley, and chopped garlic clove in a mixing bowl.
- Add the turkey fillet and chicken stock; stir it. Leave the mixture for 10 minutes to marinate.
- Take your Instant Pot; open the top lid. Plug it and turn it on.
- Press "SAUTe" setting, add the ghee and the pot will start heating up.
- Add the chicken mix. Close the top lid and seal its valve.
- Press "POULTRY" setting. Adjust cooking time to 15 minutes.
- Allow the recipe to cook for the set cooking time.

- After the set cooking time ends, press "CANCEL" and then press "QPR (Quick Pressure Release)".
- Instant Pot will quickly release the pressure.
- Open the top lid, add the cooked recipe mix in serving plates.
- Serve and enjoy!

Nutrition:

- Calories - 286
- Fat - 12.5g
- Carbs - 2.5g
- Protein - 43.5g

SWEET CHICKEN LEG STEW

Serving: 4

Ingredients:

- 4 medium-sized chicken legs
- 1 cup diced canned tomatoes; sugar-free
- 2 garlic cloves; whole
- 1 red bell pepper; chopped
- 2 cups mushrooms; sliced
- 3 tablespoon fresh parsley
- 2 tablespoon balsamic vinegar
- 3 tablespoon avocado oil
- 1 onion; finely chopped
- 3 celery stalks; chopped.
- 4 cups chicken broth
- 1 teaspoon dried oregano
- 1/4 teaspoon red pepper flakes

- 2 tablespoon fresh basil; finely chopped
- 1 teaspoon black pepper
- 1 teaspoon fresh thyme; finely chopped
- 1 teaspoon salt

Directions:

- Place the meat in a large colander and rinse thoroughly under cold running water. Dry with a kitchen paper and rub each piece with salt and pepper
- Plug in the instant pot and press the "SAUTE" button. Heat the oil and add chicken thighs in a couple of batches. Brown on all sides, for 3-4 minutes. Remove from the pot and set aside.
- In a deep bowl, combine onions, peppers, celery stalks, and mushrooms. Season with some salt and mix well. Now add garlic and season with oregano and red pepper flakes. Toss well to combine and continue to cook for another 2 minutes.
- Finally, add the remaining ingredients and seal the lid
- Set the steam release handle to the "SEALING" position and press the "MANUAL" button. Set the timer for 15 minutes on high pressure
- When done, perform a quick release and open the lid. Serve and enjoy.

Nutrition:

- Calories - 267
- Fat - 6.5g
- Carbs - 7.7g

- Protein - 40.2g

TURKEY BREAST WITH GARLIC GRAVY RECIPE

Serving: 6

Ingredients:

- 3 -pounds turkey breast; boneless and skinless
- 1 large onion; finely chopped
- 2 cups chicken stock
- 1/2 teaspoon garlic powder
- 1/4 smoked paprika
- 1 teaspoon onion powder
- 1 celery stalk; finely chopped
- 4 tablespoon butter
- 3 garlic cloves; crushed
- 1 thyme sprig; whole
- 1 sea salt

Directions:

- In a small bowl, combine salt, garlic powder, onion powder, and smoked paprika, Set aside
- Rinse the meat and place on a clean work surface. Using a sharp knife, slice each piece lengthwise to create a pocket. Stuff each with celery, garlic, and onions. Generously run with spices and Pour in the stock and add thyme sprig. Seal the lid and set the steam release handle to the "SEALING"position.
- Press the "MANUAL" button and set the timer for 20 minutes on high pressure

- When done, release the pressure naturally and open the lid. Stir in the butter and let it sit, covered, for a while before serving

Nutrition:

- Calories - 320
- Fat - 11.7g
- Carbs - 10.9g
- Protein - 39.3g

SIMPLE ONION CHICKEN

Serving: 6

Ingredients:

- 2 cups yellow onions, sliced
- 2 cups mushrooms, quartered
- ¼ cup butter, cubed
- 2 cups green beans, trimmed
- 1 ½ pounds bone-in chicken pieces
- 1 teaspoon salt
- 1 teaspoon black pepper
- 1 tablespoon fresh thyme
- 1 sprig fresh rosemary
- ½ lemon, cut into wedges
- ½ cup almonds, sliced

Directions:

- Layer the onions and mushrooms in the bottom of a slow cooker.

- Dot the onions and mushrooms with the cubed butter.
- Place the green beans on top.
- Next, add the chicken and season with salt, black pepper, thyme, and rosemary.
- Pour in the chicken stock and add the lemon wedges to the slow cooker.
- Cover and cook for 8 hours.
- Garnish with sliced almonds before serving.

Nutrition:

- Calories - 287.5
- Fat - 14.8 g
- Carbs - 9.7 g
- Protein - 29.5 g

LEMON MUSTARD CHICKEN WITH POTATOES

Serving: 6-8

Ingredients:

- 2 lbs chicken thighs
- 2 tbsp olive oil
- 3 lbs red potatoes, peeled and quartered
- 2 tbsp Italian seasoning
- 3 tbsp Dijon mustard
- ¾ cup chicken broth
- ¼ cup lemon juice
- 1 tsp salt
- 1 tsp ground black pepper

Directions:

- Select the SAUTe setting on the Instant Pot and heat the oil.
- Add the chicken thighs to the pot and saute for 2-3 minutes, until starting to brown.
- Add the potatoes, Italian seasoning, and Dijon mustard. Cook, stir occasionally, for 2 minutes.
- Pour the broth and lemon juice into the pot, stir.
- Season with salt and pepper. Close and lock the lid.
- Press the CANCEL button to reset the cooking program. Select the POULTRY setting and set the cooking time for 15 minutes.
- When the timer beeps, let the pressure Release Naturally for 10 minutes, then release any remaining steam manually. Carefully unlock the lid.
- Serve.

LIME CHICKEN DRUMSTICKS

Serving: 7

Ingredients:

- 3 oz garlic
- 17 oz chicken drumsticks
- 1 lime
- 1 teaspoon lemon zest
- 1 teaspoon kosher salt
- 1 teaspoon coriander
- 1 teaspoon butter

Directions:

- Peel the garlic cloves and mash them.
- Chop the lime into the small pieces and combine with the lemon zest.
- Add kosher salt and coriander. Add the lime to the spices and mix.
- Butter the slow cooker carefully and add the chicken drumsticks. Sprinkle the poultry with the lime mixture. Close the lid and cook the chicken on HIGH for 3.5 hours.
- Serve the chicken drumsticks immediately.
- Enjoy!

Nutrition:

- Calories - 136
- Fat - 7
- Carbs - 4.68
- Protein - 13

BARBECUE SWEET GOLD CHICKEN DRUMSTICKS

Serving: 4

Ingredients:

- 1 large sweet onion, cut into ¾-inch thick slices
- 2½ pounds chicken drumsticks, skinned
- 1 cup barbecue sauce
- 2 tablespoons orange marmalade
- 2 tablespoons yellow mustard
- Salt and pepper

- Olive oil
- 1 tablespoon of lemon pepper seasoning

Directions:

- Generously brush the bottom and sides of the slow cooker with olive oil.
- Place the sliced onion on the bottom.
- Add chicken on top of the onions. Season with salt and pepper.
- For the sauce: Stir together BBQ sauce, marmalade, and mustard in a small bowl.
- Add the sauce on top of the chicken.
- Cover and cook on LOW for 6-8 hours or on HIGH for 3-4 hours.
- Serve chicken with sauce.

Nutrition:

- Calories - 456
- Fat - 17 g
- Carbs - 37 g
- Protein - 38 g

PORK, BEEF AND LAMB

BUTTER LAMB SHOULDER

Serving: 5

Ingredients:

- 2 lbs lamb shoulder, chopped
- 3 tbsp butter

- 2 cups beef broth
- ½ eggplant, cubed
- 4 garlic cloves, crushed
- 1 tomato, chopped
- Spices: 1 ½ tsp salt
- 1 tsp black pepper, ground
- 2 tsp cumin powder
- 2 tsp coriander powder
- 1 tsp onion powder
- 1 tbsp ginger, freshly grated
- 1 cinnamon stick

Directions:

- In a small bowl, combine salt, black pepper, cumin powder, coriander powder, and grated ginger.
- Set aside.
- Rinse well the meat and rub with spices.
- Set aside.
- Plug in the instant pot and press the "Saute" button. Grease the inner pot with butter and heat up. Add meat, in several batches, and cook for 4-5 minutes, turning once.
- Remove from the pot and set aside.
- Now add eggplant and garlic. Season with some salt and cook for 5 minutes, stirring constantly. Add tomatoes and give it a good stir. Continue to cook for another minute.
- Now add the meat and pour in the broth.
- Seal the lid.
- Set the steam release handle to the "Sealing" position and press the "MANUAL" button.
- Cook for 25 minutes on high pressure.

- When done, release the pressure naturally and open the lid.
- Serve immediately.
- Optionally, use the "Slow Cooker" mode and cook for 8 hours on low.

Nutrition:

- Calories - 431
- Fat - 20.9g
- Carbs - 2.5g
- Protein - 53.7g

LAMB CURRY

Serving: 4

Ingredients:

- 1 tablespoon coconut oil
- 1 ½ - 2 pounds boneless lamb shoulder, cut into bite-size pieces
- 1 ½ teaspoons ghee or coconut oil
- 1 ½ tablespoons ginger, grated
- 1 large onion, chopped
- 4 cloves garlic, minced
- 2 ½ teaspoons garam masala or curry powder of choice
- 1 teaspoon turmeric
- 2 Roma or plum tomatoes, diced
- 1 ½ cups coconut milk
- 1 cup water or broth (vegetable or meat broth
- 1 teaspoon sea salt

- 2 cups of vegetables of your choice, such as broccoli, cauliflower, celery or carrots, cut into chunks
- 1 cinnamon stick
- 1 bay leaf
- 1 tablespoon lime or lemon juice
- red pepper flakes, (or to taste)
- ⅛ cup coconut cream (optional)
- cilantro, chopped, for garnish

Directions:

- Heat the coconut oil in a skillet over a high heat.
- Add the lamb pieces and sear until browned on the edges (for about 3-5 minutes).
- Reduce the heat and add the ghee or coconut oil.
- Stir in the ginger, garlic, and onion and cook until fragrant (for about 1 minute).
- Add the curry powder and turmeric, tomatoes and salt. Allow it to cook to release flavors (for about 2 minutes).
- Pour in the coconut milk and water. Bring to a boil.
- Carefully Add the vegetables, cinnamon stick, and bay leaf.
- Cook for 3 ½ to 4 hours on HIGH or 8 to 9 hours on LOW. The lamb should be tender.
- Drizzle with dried pepper flakes and lime juice.
- Serve garnished with cilantro and coconut cream (optional).

Nutrition:

- Calories - 394
- Fat - 20.3 g
- Carbs - 14.7 g
- Protein - 36.3 g

CHEESY CHILI RECIPE

Serving: 4

Ingredients:

- 1 pound ground beef, browned, drained
- 2 packets chili seasoning
- 2 cans (14½ ounces each tomatoes with chipotle chilies, diced
- ¾ pound elbow macaroni
- Cheese, grated and sour cream
- (optional)

Directions:

- Mix the first three ingredients in your slow cooker.
- Cook on LOW for 8 hours.
- When the beef is almost done, cook the pasta and add it to the crockpot.
- Let everything cook for another half hour.

Nutrition:

- Calories - 130
- Fat - 33 g

- Carbs - 21 g
- Protein - 3 g

SPICY LAMB

Serving: 6

Ingredients:

- 2 lbs boneless leg of lamb, cut into bite-sized pieces
- ¼ cup heavy cream
- 2 tbsp ghee
- 2 cups cherry tomatoes, chopped
- 3 cups vegetable stock
- Spices: 1 tsp salt
- 1 tbsp coriander powder
- 1 tsp ginger powder
- 1 tsp cumin powder
- 2 tbsp chili powder
- 1 tsp garam masala
- ½ tsp garlic powder
- 2 tsp fennel seeds
- 1 ½ tsp cumin seeds
- 3 cloves, whole
- 1 cinnamon stick
- 3 bay leaves

Directions:

- Rinse the meat under cold running water and pat dry with a kitchen paper. Place on a clean work surface and chop into bite-sized pieces. Place in a deep bowl and add heavy cream and garam masala. Stir well and tightly wrap with aluminum foil. Refrigerate overnight.

- Plug in the instant pot and press the "Saute" button. Grease the inner pot with ghee and add bay leaves, cardamom, cinnamon, cloves, cumin seeds, and fennel seeds. Briefly cook for 1-2 minutes, stirring constantly with a wooden spatula.
- Now add the remaining spices and stir well again. Continue to cook for another minute.
- Finally, add the meat along with the heavy cream. Pour in the stock and add cherry tomatoes. Stir well and seal the lid. Set the steam release handle and press the "MANUAL" button.
- Set the timer for 25 minutes on high pressure.
- When done, release the pressure naturally and open the lid. Stir well again and serve immediately.

Nutrition:

- Calories - 350
- Fat - 17.4g
- Carbs - 1.9g
- Protein - 43.3g

TOMATO LAMB WITH BRUSSELS SPROUTS

Serving: 4

Ingredients:

- 2 racks of lamb
- 1 cup Brussels sprouts
- 1 cup cherry tomatoes, whole
- ½ cup button mushrooms
- 2 celery stalks
- 2 tbsp olive oil
- 3 cups vegetable stock
- 1 cup sour cream
- Spices: 1 tsp salt
- ½ tsp black pepper, freshly ground
- ½ tsp chili powder
- ½ tsp dried sage
- 1 tsp dried rosemary

Directions:

- Rinse the lamb under cold running water and sprinkle with salt, rosemary, and sage. Place at the bottom of the instant pot and pour in the stock.
- Seal the lid and set the steam release handle to the "Sealing" position. Press the "MANUAL" button and set the timer for 15 minutes on high pressure.
- When done, perform a quick pressure release and open the lid.

- Now add sprouts, tomatoes, mushrooms, celery stalks, and oil. Season with some more salt, and chili powder.
- Seal the lid again and continue to cook for another 5 minutes on the "MANUAL" mode.
- Carefully open the lid when done and serve with sour cream.

Nutrition:

- Calories - 487
- Fat - 30.3g
- Carbs - 5.4g
- Protein - 45.7g

FRUITED BBQ PORK CHOPS

Serving: 6

Ingredients:

- 6 boneless 1-inch thick pork chops
- 1 teaspoon dried thyme, crushed
- 2 7-ounce packages mixed dried fruit
- 1 medium red or yellow bell pepper, seeded and sliced
- 1 cup bottled barbecue sauce

Directions:

- Trim some fat from pork chops.
- Brown pork in a sprayed skilled over medium-high heat.

- Place chops in the slow cooker and sprinkle with thyme.
- Add dried fruit and sweet pepper. Pour barbecue sauce over pork chops.
- Cover and cook for 4 to 4 ½ hours on LOW or for 2 to 2 ½ hours on HIGH.
- Serve drizzled with the cooking juices from the slow cooker.

Nutrition:

- Calories - 450
- Fat - 11 g
- Carbs - 49 g
- Protein - 40 g

CURRIED LAMB WITH ZUCCHINI AND TOMATOES

Serving: 4

Ingredients:

- 1 tbsp. Ghee
- 2 tsp minced Garlic
- 1 pound Lab, cut into cubes
- 1 tsp grated Ginger
- 1 cup diced Tomatoes
- ½ cup Coconut Milk
- 1 Zucchini, diced
- 1 Onion, diced
- 1 Carrot, thinly sliced
- 1 ½ tbsp. Curry Powder

Directions:

- Place the lamb, ginger, garlic, and coconut milk, in a bowl.
- Cover and place in the fridge to marinate for 3 hours.
- Add the carrot, onion, tomatoes, and ghee.
- Close the lid and cook for 20 minutes on HIGH.
- Do a natural pressure release.
- Stir in the zucchini and cook on SAUTE for 5-6 more minutes.
- Serve and enjoy!

Nutrition:

- Calories - 338
- Fat - 21g
- Carbs - 7.5g
- Protein - 23g

PORK BUTT ROAST

Serving: 5

Ingredients:

- 2 -pounds pork butt; sliced
- 2 cups cauliflower; chopped into florets
- 2 large tomatoes; sliced
- 4 tablespoon olive oil
- 3 tablespoon butter
- 2 large onions; sliced
- 4 cups beef broth
- 1/2 teaspoon nutmeg

- 1 teaspoon freshly ground black pepper
- 1 ½ teaspoon salt

Directions:

- Rub the meat with olive oil and season with salt, pepper, and nutmeg. Place in the instant pot and pour in the broth
- Seal the lid and set the steam release handle to the "SEALING" position. Press the "MANUAL" button and cook for 20 minutes on high pressure.
- Meanwhile, preheat the oven to 400 degrees. Brush a baking pan with butter and set aside
- When you hear the cooker's end signal, perform a quick pressure release and open the lid. Pour in about one cup of the broth and roast for about 15-20 minutes or until the meat is lightly charred and the vegetables fork-tender.

Nutrition:

- Calories - 494
- Fat - 25.8g
- Carbs - 8.1g
- Protein - 53.5g

AMAZING MEDITERRANEAN PORK

Serving: 6

Ingredients:

- 3 pounds pork shoulder, boneless
- For the marinade: ¼ cup olive oil
- 2 teaspoons oregano, dried
- ¼ cup lemon juice
- 2 teaspoons mustard
- 2 teaspoons minutes
- 6 garlic cloves, minced
- 2 teaspoons Paleo pesto sauce
- Black pepper to the taste
- A pinch of sea salt

Directions:

- In a bowl, mix oil with lemon juice, oregano, mint, mustard, garlic, pesto, salt and pepper and stir very well.
- Rub pork shoulder with the marinade, cover and keep in the fridge for 10 hours.
- Flip pork shoulder and keep in the fridge for 10 more hours.
- Slice roast and serve with a tasty side salad!
- Enjoy!

Nutrition:

- Calories - 300
- Fat - 4

- Carbs - 7
- Protein - 10

PORK LEG ROAST RECIPE

Serving: 6

Ingredients:

- 3 -pounds pork leg
- 2 spring onions; finely chopped
- 2 tablespoon mustard
- 3 tablespoon soy sauce
- 4 tablespoon olive oil
- 1 teaspoon coriander seeds
- 1/2 teaspoon dried sage
- 1/2 teaspoon dried rosemary
- 2 bay leaves
- 1 teaspoon white peppercorn

Directions:

- Grease the inner pot with two tablespoons of olive oil and press the "SAUTE" button. Heat up and add spring onions and coriander seeds. Cook for 2-3 minutes and then add the meat.
- Pour in 5-6 cups of water and add bay leaves. Seal the lid. Set the steam release handle to the "SEALING" position and press the "MEAT" button
- Cook for 25 minutes on high pressure.
- When done, release the pressure naturally and open the lid. Remove the meat from the pot and chill for a while

- Preheat the oven to 450 degrees F. Grease a baking sheet with the remaining oil and set aside
- Rub the meat with sage and rosemary and place on a baking sheet. Pour in about one cup of water.
- Place in the oven and reduce the heat to 400. Roast for 20 minutes.

Nutrition:

- Calories - 428
- Fat - 18.4g
- Carbs - 1.6g
- Protein - 60.9g

FIVE SPICE RIBS WITH SAVOY CABBAGE

Serving: 6

Ingredients:

- 2 pounds pork ribs, cut into sections
- 1 teaspoon salt
- 1 teaspoon black pepper
- 1 tablespoon tomato paste
- 1 tablespoon soy sauce
- 2 tablespoons rice vinegar
- 4 cloves garlic, crushed and minced
- 1 tablespoon jalapeño pepper, diced
- 1 tablespoon five spice powder
- 1 cup onions, sliced
- 3 cups savoy cabbage, sliced
- 1 cup full fat coconut milk

Directions:

- Season the ribs with salt and black pepper and set them aside.
- In a bowl, combine the tomato paste, soy sauce, rice vinegar, garlic, jalapeño, and five spice powder. Mix well.
- Place the cabbage in the bottom of the slow cooker, along with the coconut milk.
- Next, using a basting brush, spread the sauce over the ribs until they are completely coated.
- Place the ribs in the slow cooker.
- Cover and cook on low for 10 hours.

Nutrition:

- Calories - 589.8
- Fat - 45.5 g
- Carbs - 5.5 g
- Protein - 37.9 g

RED WINE BRAISED BEEF BRISKET

Serving: 4-6

Ingredients:

- 3 lbs beef brisket, flat cut
- 3 tbsp olive oil
- 1 tsp kosher salt
- 1 tsp ground black pepper
- 1 large onion, sliced
- 1 carrot, chopped

- 1 stalk celery, diced
- 1 tbsp tomato paste
- 2 cloves garlic, minced
- 1 cup beef broth
- 1 cup red wine
- 2 sprigs fresh thyme
- 1 bay leaf

Directions:

- Select the SAUTe setting on the Instant Pot and heat the oil (2 tablespoons.
- Rub all sides of the beef brisket with salt and pepper.
- Put the beef in the pot and brown the meat for 4-5 minutes on each side.
- Pour in 1 tablespoon of oil and add onion, carrot, celery, and tomato paste.
- Saute for 4-5 minutes.
- Add the garlic and cook for another 30-45 seconds.
- Pour in the broth and red wine and deglaze the pot by scraping the bottom to remove all of the brown bits.
- Return the meat to the pot and add thyme and bay leaf.
- Press the CANCEL key to stop the SAUTe function.
- Close and lock the lid. Select MANUAL and cook at HIGH pressure for 60 minutes.
- Once timer goes off, allow to
- Naturally Release
- for 10 minutes. Then release any remaining pressure manually.

- Uncover the pot.
- Press the SAUTE key and simmer until the sauce thickens.
- Serve the brisket with sauce.

BBQ BEEF TENDERLOINS

Serving: 6

Ingredients:

- 3-pound beef tenderloin
- ½ teaspoon paprika
- 1 teaspoon cayenne pepper
- ½ teaspoon sumac
- ½ teaspoon salt
- ½ teaspoon dried oregano
- 1 teaspoon ground ginger
- 2 tablespoons tomato paste
- 3 teaspoons olive oil
- ½ teaspoon onion powder
- 1 teaspoon minced garlic
- ¼ cup of water

Directions:

- Make BBQ sauce: mix up together paprika, cayenne pepper, sumac, salt, dried oregano, ground ginger, tomato paste, olive oil, onion powder, and minced garlic.
- Spread the beef tenderloin with prepared BBQ sauce well and Add remaining BBQ sauce if there is.
- Then add water and close the lid.

- Cook beef tenderloin for 9 hours on Low.
- Then slice the meat and sprinkle it with "meat juice" from the crockpot.

Nutrition:

- Calories - 496
- Fat - 23.2
- Carbs - 1.9
- Protein - 66.1

MEATLOAF RECIPE

Serving: 6

Ingredients:

- 2 lbs. ground pork
- 1 cup almond flour
- 2 small onions, finely chopped
- 2 spring onions, finely chopped
- ½ cup celery stalk, finely chopped
- 3 garlic cloves, crushed
- 2 tbsps. butter
- 3 tbsps. olive oil
- 1 cup cherry tomatoes, chopped.
- 2 tsps. dried celery
- ½ tsp. white pepper; ground
- 1 tsp. salt

Directions:

- In a large bowl, combine the ground pork with onions, spring onions, celery stalk, and garlic. Sprinkle with salt, celery, and pepper.
- Now add about one cup of almond flour and mix well again. Optionally, add a handful of finely chopped almonds for a crunchy taste. a large piece of plastic foil and wrap tightly. Refrigerate for 30 minutes.
- Meanwhile; place cherry tomatoes in a food processor and process until smooth. Add olive oil and mix well. Set aside.
- Remove the meat from the refrigerator and place back in the mixing bowl. Add tomatoes and butter. Mix well again and shape the meatloaf using a large piece of plastic foil. Place in a baking dish and loosely cover with aluminum foil.
- Plug in the Instant Pot and set the trivet at the bottom of the inner pot. Pour in one cup of water and place the baking dish on top.
- Seal the lid and set the steam release handle to the "Sealing" position. Press the "MANUAL" button and set the timer for 20 minutes on high pressure.
- When done, perform a quick pressure release and open the lid. Remove the pan from the pot and chill for a while.
- Serve and enjoy!

Nutrition:

- Calories - 358
- Fat - 18.5g
- Protein - 41.4g

- Carbs - 4.0g
- Sugar - 0.1g

PORK ROAST WITH WALNUT BRUSSELS SPROUTS

Serving: 8

Ingredients:

- 4 cups Brussels sprouts, halved
- 4 cloves garlic, crushed and minced
- ½ cup pancetta, cubed
- 2 tablespoons olive oil
- 1 teaspoon salt
- 1 teaspoon black pepper
- 2 teaspoons rubbed sage
- 1 fresh rosemary sprig
- 2 pounds pork tenderloin roast
- 1 cup chicken stock
- ½ cup walnuts, chopped
- ½ cup Brie cheese

Directions:

- Place the Brussels sprouts, garlic, and pancetta in the slow cooker. Drizzle with the olive oil and season with salt, black pepper, rubbed sage, and rosemary. Toss to mix.
- Add the tenderloin roast to the slow cooker, and pour in the chicken stock.
- Cover and cook on low for 8 hours.
- Remove the tenderloin from the slow cooker and allow it to rest before slicing.

- Meanwhile, add the walnuts and Brie cheese. Mix well, cover and cook an additional 10 minutes before serving.

Nutrition:

- Calories - 407.2
- Fat - 24.5 g
- Carbs - 5.1 g
- Protein - 41 g

ASIAN PORK STRIPS

Serving: 4

Ingredients:

- 1-pound pork neck; cut into 2-inch long strips
- 1/2 cup canned bamboo; chopped.
- 2 red bell peppers; sliced into strips
- 2 tablespoon dark soy sauce
- 1 spring onion; finely chopped.
- 2 tablespoon light soy sauce
- 1 tablespoon rice vinegar
- 1-egg
- 3 tablespoon vegetable oil
- 1/2 teaspoon stevia powder
- 1/2 teaspoon salt

Directions:

- Rinse the meat and place on a large cutting board. Using a sharp knife, cut into strips and place in a deep bowl. Add one egg, salt, and soy

sauce. Cover with a lid and set it sit for 10-15 minutes
- Plug in the instant pot and press the "SAUTE" button. Add half of the meat and cook for 6-7 minutes, stirring constantly. Repeat with the remaining meat and remove from the pot, Set aside.
- Now; grease the inner pot with oil and heat up. Add bamboo and sliced bell peppers. Cook for 7-8 minutes, stirring constantly
- Sprinkle with stevia and rice vinegar and add the meat. Give it a good stir and add onions
- Continue to cook for another 2-3 minutes. Press the "CANCEL" button and serve immediately

Nutrition:

- Calories - 302
- Fat - 15.5g
- Carbs - 5.3g
- Protein - 33g

INSTANT POT CARNE GUISADA

Serving: 4

Ingredients:

- 2 tablespoons olive oil
- 1 onion, diced
- 1 tablespoon minced garlic
- 1-pound beef stew meat
- 1 serrano peppers, minced
- 1 bay leaf

- 1 ground cu minutes
- 1 teaspoon chili powder
- 1 teaspoon paprika
- Salt and pepper
- 1 cup beef stock
- ½ cup tomato sauce

Directions:

- Press the Saute button on the Instant Pot.
- Heat the oil and saute the onion and garlic.
- Add in the beef stew meat and stir for another 3 minutes until lightly brown.
- Stir in the rest of the ingredients. Mix well to combine.
- Close the lid and press the Meat/Stew button.
- Adjust the cooking time to 40 minutes.
- Do natural pressure release.

Nutrition:

- Calories - 411
- Carbs - 12.6g
- Protein - 37.8g
- Fat - 22.2g

LEMON BEEF MEAL

Serving: 2

Ingredients:

- 2 tablespoons lemon juice
- 1 garlic clove, crushed

- 1 tablespoon oil
- 2 beef steaks, about 3 ½ ounce each
- ½ teaspoon garlic salt

Directions:

- Take your Instant Pot and place over dry kitchen surface; open its top lid and switch it on.
- Press "SAUTe".
- In its cooking pot, add and heat the oil.
- Add the meat and salt; stir-cook for 4-5 minutes to evenly brown.
- Add the garlic and cook for 1-2 minutes.
- Serve with lemon juice on top.

Nutrition:

- Calories - 86
- Fat - 7g
- Carbs - 2g
- Sodium - 427mg
- Protein - 2g

CREAMY BEEF STEW

Serving: 5

Ingredients:

- Cooking spray1 ½ pounds beef round, cut in 1" pieces
- 2 packets of frozen vegetables (16 ounces each
- 1 can of condensed cream of mushroom soup
- 1 can of condensed tomato soup

- 1 envelope onion soup mix

Directions:

- Coat a skillet with the cooking spray and brown the meat on all sides.
- Place the vegetables and meat in the slow cooker.
- Combine the remaining ingredients in a separate bowl and pour over the meat and vegetables.
- Stir and cover.
- Set on LOW and cook for 6-8 hours, or until the meat is tender.

Nutrition:

- Calories - 415
- Fat - 13 g
- Carbs - 41 g
- Protein - 30 g

CRANBERRY MAPLE ORANGE PORK CHOPS

Serving: 5

Ingredients:

- 4 tablespoons coconut oil
- 1 ½ pounds pork chop, bone in
- 1 onion, diced
- ½ cup orange juice
- ¼ cup maple syrup
- 1 ½ teaspoon cinnamon
- 1 teaspoon garlic cloves

- 1/3 cup cranberries
- 2 teaspoons rosemary, fresh
- Salt and pepper

Directions:

- Press the Saute button on the Instant Pot.
- Heat the oil and place the pork chops. Sear on all sides.
- Stir in the rest of the ingredients. Scrape the bottom to remove the browning.
- Close the lid and press the Meat/Stew button.
- Adjust the cooking time to 60 minutes.
- Do natural pressure release.

Nutrition:

- Calories - 388
- Carbs - 3.2g
- Protein - 45g
- Fat - 29g

LAYERED BRISKET DINNER WITH TANGY MUSTARD SAUCE

Serving: 4

Ingredients:

- For tangy mustard sauce
- ¼ cup light sour cream
- ¼ tsp dried Italian seasoning, crushed
- ¾ tsp Dijon style mustard
- ¼ tsp snipped fresh thyme (optional

- For Layered brisket
- 1 ½ lb fresh beef brisket, trimmed of fat
- ½ Tbsp Worcestershire sauce
- Pepper to taste
- 4 oz baby carrots
- 1 tsp olive oil
- Salt to taste
- Snipped fresh thyme (optional)
- ½ Tbsp Dijon style mustard
- ½ Tbsp balsamic vinegar
- ½ lb baby potatoes, red or yellow, halved if large
- ½ small onion, cut into wedges
- ¼ tsp dried Italian seasoning, crushed

Directions:

- For tangy mustard sauce: Whisk together sour cream, thyme, Italian seasoning and mustard in a bowl.
- Cover and refrigerate until use.
- For layered brisket: Lay the brisket in the slow cooker.
- Add mustard, vinegar, pepper powder and Worcestershire sauce into a small bowl and whisk well. Spread the sauce mixture over the brisket. Turn the brisket and spread the sauce mixture on the other side of the brisket.
- Take a large sheet of heavy foil. Lay carrots, potato and onion over it. Pour oil over the vegetables and toss well. Season with salt, pepper and Italian seasoning. Seal completely and place in the slow cooker, over the brisket.
- Cover the pot and cook for 8-9 hours on Low.

- Remove brisket from the pot and place on your cutting board. When cool enough to handle, cut into slices or shred with a pair of forks. Unfold the foil packet just before serving.
- Serve brisket slices topped with the vegetables. Serve with tangy mustard sauce. Garnish with thyme and serve.

Nutrition:

- Calories - 273

CHEESEY MEATBALLS

Serving: 6

Ingredients:

- 2 -pounds lean ground beef
- 1 tablespoon fresh parsley; finely chopped
- 1 small Jalapeno pepper; chopped.
- 1 tablespoon butter
- 1 tablespoon Dijon mustard
- 3-ounce cheddar cheese
- 2 large eggs; beaten
- 2 garlic cloves; crushed
- 1 cup beef stock
- 1/4 teaspoon smoked paprika; ground.
- 1/2 teaspoon black pepper; ground.
- 1 teaspoon salt

Directions:

- In a large mixing bowl, combine ground beef, cheese, eggs, garlic, Jalapeno pepper, parsley, mustard, paprika, salt, and pepper
- Mix until well incorporated
- Shape the meatballs, about 1 to 1 ½ -inch in diameter and set aside
- Plug in the instant pot and add butter to the stainless steel insert. Gently melt over the "SAUTE" mode, stirring constantly
- Spread the meatballs on the bottom of the pot and slowly pour in the beef stock.
- Securely lock the lid and set the steam release the handle by moving the valve to the "SEALING" position.
- Press the "MANUAL" button and set the timer for 10 minutes. Cook on "HIGH" pressure
- When done, perform a quick release of the pressure and open the pot.
- Optionally, garnish with some finely chopped cilantro before serving.

Nutrition:

- Calories - 387
- Fat - 17.9g
- Carbs - 0.9g
- Protein - 52.2g

CHILI WITH BEEF AND CHORIZO

Serving: 6

Ingredients:

- 1 ½ tablespoon olive oil or coconut oil
- 7 -ounce chorizo sausage; peeled and diced.
- 1 long red chili; finely diced.
- 1 large brown onion; chopped
- 1 carrot; peeled, diced into small cubes
- 1 celery stick; diced into small cubes
- 2.2-pound ground beef
- 3 cloves garlic; diced.
- 2 teaspoon ground cu minutes
- 2 teaspoon ground coriander seed
- 2 cups canned chopped tomatoes
- 4 tablespoon tomato paste
- 1 tablespoon Tamari or soy sauce
- 2 teaspoon salt
- 2 bay leaves
- 3 tablespoon port or fortified red wine

Directions:

- Turn the Instant Pot on and press the "SAUTE" function key. Add the oil, onion, carrot, celery, chorizo, and chili. Cook for 3-4 minutes
- Stir in the beef, garlic, spices, canned tomatoes, and paste. Stir. Add the remaining ingredients and stir together. Press "KEEP WARM/CANCEL" *
- Put on and lock the lid, make sure the steam releasing handle is pointing to "SEALING" Press

"MANUAL" (High Pressure) and set to 15 minutes
- Let the pressure release for 5 minutes, and then use the quick release to let off the rest of the steam. Serve hot

Nutrition:

- Calories - 346
- Carbs - 7.3 g
- Carbs - 2.5 g
- Fat - 26 g
- Protein - 21g

ROSEMARY LAMB

Serving: 6-8

Ingredients:

- 4 lbs lamb, boneless and cut into 1-2 inch cubes
- Salt and ground black pepper to taste
- 2 tbsp olive oil
- 4 cloves garlic, minced
- 3 tbsp flour
- 1½ cups veggie stock
- 1 cup carrots, sliced
- 4 rosemary sprigs

Directions:

- Season the lamb with salt and pepper to taste.
- Preheat the Instant Pot by selecting SAUTe. Add and heat the oil.

- Add the garlic and saute for 1 minute.
- Add the lamb and cook until browned, stirring occasionally. You may have to do it in two batches.
- Add the flour and stir. Pour over the stock.
- Add the carrots and rosemary. Close and lock the lid.
- Press the CANCEL key to stop the SAUTe function.
- Select MANUAL and cook at HIGH pressure for 25 minutes.
- Once cooking is complete, use a Natural Release for 10 minutes, then release any remaining pressure manually. Open the lid.
- Remove the rosemary stems.
- Serve the lamb with sauce.

PORK CHOPS WITH CREAMY HERB SAUCE

Serving: 2

Ingredients:

- 1/3 cup chicken broth
- 1/4 cup heavy cream
- 1/2 lb pork chops (bone-in, browned
- Herbs and spices of choice (basil, parsley, mustard, thyme, garlic, pepper, onion)

Directions:

- Sprinkle each side of pork chops with the spices of choice.

- Place pork chops in a crock-pot and add chicken broth..
- Cover and cook on high for 3-4 hours.
- Remove pork chops from crock-pot and set aside.
- Carefully whisk cream in the unwashed crock-pot. Add additional salt and pepper to taste.
- Bring the contents to a boil while stirring continuously.

Nutrition:

- Calories - 582
- Fat - 38g
- Carbs - 5g
- Protein - 50g
- Cholesterol - 220mg
- Sodium - 765mg
- Serving suggestions: Pour the sauce over pork chops. Garnish it with remaining dried herbs.
- Tip: About 1 tbsp cornstarch can be added while cooking the cream to make it thicker.

MEXICAN BEEF ROAST

Serving: 6

Ingredients:

- 6 garlic cloves, crushed
- ½ cup roasted tomato salsa
- ½ cup bone broth
- 2 ½ pounds beef chuck roast, cut into small pieces
- 1 tablespoon butter (melted

- 2 teaspoons salt
- 1 teaspoon fish sauce
- 1 tablespoon chili powder
- 1 onion, thinly cut into slices
- 1 tablespoon tomato paste
- 1 teaspoon black pepper (ground)

Directions:

- Season the beef with the chili powder and salt.
- Take your Instant Pot and open the top lid.
- Add the butter and heat it; saute the onions until Add the tomato paste and garlic and cook until fragrant, stirring frequently.
- Add the beef and remaining ingredients and stir the mix.
- Close the top lid and seal the pressure valve.
- Press "MEAT" setting with 35 minutes of cooking time and "HIGH" pressure mode.
- Press "NPR" function to release the pressure slowly in a natural way.
- Open the lid; Enjoy!

Nutrition:

- Calories - 116
- Fat - 3g
- Carbs - 4g
- Sodium - 746mg
- Protein - 21g

AMAZING PULLED PORK

Serving: 8

Ingredients:

- 5 pounds pork shoulder
- 2 cups tomato puree
- 6 Medjool Dates, pitted
- ½ teaspoon cloves, ground
- ½ teaspoon cinnamon
- 2 teaspoons salt
- Extra virgin olive oil
- Tortilla Wraps
- 8 eggs
- 1 tablespoon coconut flour
- ½ teaspoon salt

Directions:

- Place pitted dates in blender, and mix until paste forms, add tomato puree, cinnamon, salt, black pepper, and mix.
- Combine mustard, blended tomato puree, cloves, cinnamon, salt, and mix.
- Place pork shoulder in slow cooker, pour sauce into slow cooker, and coat pork shoulder.
- Cook pork for 8 hours on high.
- Once pork is cooked, use fork to shred.
- For tortilla wraps, whisk eggs, add milk and flour, and mix until well combined.
- Heat 4 tablespoons oil in skillet on medium-high.
- Pour 1/8th of mixture into skillet and cook each side 30 seconds.

- Spoon pork mixture into egg tortilla and serve.

Nutrition:

- Calories - 777
- Fat - 55 g
- Carbs - 8 g
- Protein - 59 g

SMOKY BBQ BEEF BRISKET

Serving: 4

Ingredients:

- 2 lbs beef brisket, flat cut
- ¼ tsp garlic salt
- ¼ tsp celery salt
- 1 tsp seasoned meat tenderizer
- 2 tbsp liquid smoke
- 1 tbsp Worcestershire sauce
- ½ cup water
- 2/3 cup BBQ sauce, plus additional for serving

Directions:

- In a large bowl, combine the garlic salt, celery salt and seasoned meat tenderizer.
- Mix well.
- In the same bowl, rub all sides of the beef brisket with the spice mix. Pour the Worcestershire sauce and liquid smoke over the brisket.

- Cover the bowl tightly with aluminum foil and let marinate for at least 45 minutes or up to 9 hours in the refrigerator.
- Pour the water and BBQ sauce into the Instant Pot.
- Add the brisket and remaining liquid from the bowl to the pot.
- Close and lock the lid. Select MANUAL and cook at HIGH pressure for 50 minutes.
- When the timer beeps, let the pressure
- Release Naturally
- for 15 minutes.
- Release any remaining steam manually. Uncover the pot.

TOMATO RASAM

Serving: 5

Ingredients:

- 1 lb beef stew meat
- 2 large tomatoes, chopped
- 2 red chilies, finely chopped
- 1 small onion, finely chopped
- 4 tbsp ghee
- 2 garlic cloves, crushed
- 5 cups vegetable stock
- Spices: 2 tsp salt
- 2 tsp stevia powder
- 2 tsp turmeric powder
- 2 tsp hing
- 2 tsp mustard seeds
- 2 tsp coriander powder

- 2 tbsp chili powder

Directions:

- Plug in the instant pot and pour in the stock. Add tomatoes, onions, and chili peppers. Stir well and press the "Saute" button. Bring it to a boil and gently simmer for 15 minutes.
- Now stir in the meat and season with all spices. Add the remaining ingredients and
- stir well.
- Seal the lid and set the steam release handle to the "Sealing" position. Press the "MANUAL" button and set the timer for 40 minutes on high pressure.
- When done, release the pressure naturally and open the lid. Stir well again and serve immediately.

Nutrition:

- Calories - 285
- Fat - 16.1g
- Carbs - 5.6g
- Protein - 28.8g

CAJUN SIRLOIN

Serving: 4

Ingredients:

- 13 oz beef sirloin
- 1 tablespoon Cajun seasonings

- 1 tablespoon butter
- ½ teaspoon dried rosemary
- 1 teaspoon salt
- 1/3 cup heavy cream

Directions:

- Rub the beef sirloin with Cajun seasonings and dried rosemary.
- After this, sprinkle meat with salt and Add heavy cream and butter. Close the lid.
- Cook meat for 5.5 hours on High.

Nutrition:

- Calories - 232
- Fat - 12.3
- Carbs - 0.4
- Protein - 28.2

SNACKS AND APPETIZERS

CHICKEN PATE

Serving: 8

Ingredients:

- 1 cup vegetable stock
- 1 ½ pounds chicken livers
- A pinch of salt and black pepper
- 2 garlic cloves, minced

- 3 tablespoons olive oil
- ½ cup lemon juice

Directions:

- In your slow cooker, combine all the ingredients except the oil and the lemon juice, cover and cook on low for 5 hours.

Nutrition:

- Calories - 193
- Fat - 11,2
- Carbs - 1,6
- Protein - 21

LEMONY SNACK

Serving: 24

Ingredients:

- Cooking spray
- 1 cup walnuts, chopped
- 1 cup pumpkin seeds
- 2 tablespoons dill, dried
- 2 tablespoons olive oil
- 1 teaspoon rosemary, dried
- 1 tablespoon lemon peel, shredded

Directions:

- Grease your slow cooker with cooking spray.

- Add walnuts, pumpkin seeds, oil, dill, rosemary and lemon pee, toss, cover and cook on Low for 2 hours and 30 minutes.
- Divide nuts and seeds into bowls and serve them as a snack.
- Enjoy!

Nutrition:

- Calories - 100
- Fat - 2
- Carbs - 3
- Protein - 2

KETO QUESO DIP

Serving: 6

Ingredients:

- 1 cup ground beef
- 1 teaspoon butter
- 1 white onion, diced
- 1 cup Cheddar cheese, shredded
- ½ cup of water
- 1 teaspoon minced jalapeno pepper
- 1 tablespoon Taco seasoning

Directions:

- Put butter in the skillet and melt it.
- Add ground beef and diced onion.
- Cook the mixture for 5 minutes. Stir it from time to time.

- After this, Add shredded Cheddar cheese, jalapeno pepper, water, and Taco seasoning.
- Mix up the mixture well.
- Cook the dip on Low for 7 hours.

Nutrition:

- Calories - 134
- Fat - 9.6
- Carbs - 2.3
- Protein - 9.2

LIME CHEESECAKE

Serving: 2

Ingredients:

- 24 oz cream cheese
- 3 eggs
- 1 cup gluten-free sweetener
- ½ tbsp vanilla
- 1/4 cup lime juice

Directions:

- Mix all ingredients thoroughly using a mixer in a bowl.
- Pour 2 to 3 cups of water in the crockpot and place the bowl inside.
- Cover and cook for 2 hours and 30 minutes on high.

Nutrition:

- Calories - 219
- Fat - 16.7 g
- Carbs - 5.7 g
- Protein - 8 g
- Serving suggestions: Serve with any low-sugar fruit sauce or sliced fruits.

PEANUTS SNACK

Serving: 10

Ingredients:

- 2 pounds green peanuts
- 10 cups water
- A pinch of sea salt
- 2 tablespoons Cajun seasoning

Directions:

- In your slow cooker, mix peanuts with water, salt and Cajun seasoning, stir, cover and cook on Low for 12 hours.
- Drain, Enjoy!

Nutrition:

- Calories - 90
- Fat - 2
- Carbs - 5
- Protein - 3

CHEDDAR BACON ALE DIP

Serving: 2

Ingredients:

- 4 slices bacon, browned and diced
- 1 tbsp flour
- 3 oz amber ale
- 1 tsp Dijon mustard
- 1 cup cheddar cheese

Directions:

- Combine all ingredients in the crockpot but reserve some bacon for toppings.
- Season with salt and pepper to taste.
- Cover and cook on high for 1 hour.

Nutrition:

- Calories - 203
- Fat - 16 g
- Carbs - 3 g
- Protein - 8 g
- Serving suggestions: Top with the reserved bacon.

EASY CHEESECAKE

Serving: 2

Ingredients:

- 24 oz cream cheese
- 3 eggs
- 1 cup gluten-free sweetener
- ½ tbsp vanilla

Directions:

- Mix all ingredients thoroughly using a mixer in a bowl.
- Pour 2 to 3 cups of water in the crockpot and place the bowl inside.
- Cover and cook for 2 hours and 30 minutes on high.

Nutrition:

- Calories - 207
- Fat - 16.1 g
- Carbs - 5.7 g
- Protein - 7.8 g
- Serving suggestions: Serve with any low-sugar fruit sauce or sliced fruits.

GARLIC DIP

Serving: 7

Ingredients:

- 10 oz garlic cloves
- 5 oz Parmesan
- 1 cup cream cheese
- 1 teaspoon cayenne pepper
- 1 tablespoon dried dill
- 1 teaspoon turmeric
- ½ teaspoon butter

Directions:

- Peel the garlic cloves and place them in the slow cooker.
- Add cream cheese and cayenne pepper. Shred Parmesan cheese and add it to the slow cooker. Then sprinkle the mixture with the dried dill and turmeric.
- Add butter and close the lid. Cook the dish on LOW for 6 hours.
- After this, stir and mash the dip carefully with a wooden spatula.

Nutrition:

- Calories - 244
- Fat - 11.5
- Carbs - 23.65
- Protein - 13

MINI CHICKEN PIZZAS

Serving: 4

Ingredients:

- 1 cup ground chicken
- 1 teaspoon tomato sauce
- 1 teaspoon fresh dill, chopped
- ¼ teaspoon minced garlic
- 3 oz Parmesan, grated
- Cooking spray

Directions:

- Spray the muffin molds with cooking spray.
- Then put the ground chicken in every muffin mold and flatten to make the pizza crust.
- Brush chicken pizza crust with tomato sauce and sprinkle with minced garlic and fresh dill.
- Top every mini pizza with grated Parmesan.
- Cook the snack for 4 hours on High.

Nutrition:

- Calories - 136
- Fat - 7.2
- Carbs - 1
- Protein - 17

ALMOND CAULIFLOWER SPREAD

Serving: 4

Ingredients:

- 3 cups cauliflower florets
- ½ cup almonds, soaked overnight and drained
- 2 cups almond milk
- 1 teaspoon garlic powder

Directions:

- In your slow cooker, combine all the ingredients, cover and cook on low for 7 hours.
- Blend using an immersion blender, divide into bowls and serve.

Nutrition:

- Calories - 191
- Fat - 5
- Carbs - 11
- Protein - 6

CAULIFLOWER HUMMUS

Serving: 4

Ingredients:

- 4 tablespoons sesame seed paste
- ¼ cup vegetable stock
- 1 cauliflower head, florets separated

- 5 tablespoons olive oil
- 4 tablespoons lime juice
- 1 teaspoon garlic powder
- A pinch of salt and black pepper

Directions:

- In your slow cooker, combine all the ingredients except the sesame seed paste and the lime juice. Mix together, cover and cook on low for 4 hours.

Nutrition:

- Calories - 224
- Fat - 22,2
- Carbs - 7,2
- Protein - 3,1

MARINATED CHILI PEPPERS

Serving: 7

Ingredients:

- 2 tablespoons balsamic vinegar
- 10 oz red chili pepper
- 4 garlic cloves
- 1 white onion
- 3 tablespoons water
- 1 teaspoon oregano
- 1 teaspoon ground black pepper
- 4 tablespoons olive oil
- 1 teaspoon ground nutmeg
- ½ teaspoon ground ginger

Directions:

- Wash the chili peppers carefully and cut them across.
- After this, peel the garlic cloves and slice them. Peel the white onion and chop it.
- Combine the chopped white onion, sliced garlic cloves, water, oregano, ground black pepper, ground nutmeg, and ground ginger together. Add olive oil and whisk the mixture.
- Make a layer of the chili peppers in the slow cooker.
- Sprinkle the chili peppers with the olive oil mixture and close the lid.
- Cook the chili peppers on HIGH for 3 hours. Then let the prepared chili peppers cool. Serve the dish with the white bread toasts. Enjoy!

Nutrition:

- Calories - 96
- Fat - 8
- Carbs - 5.87
- Protein - 1

COCONUT TURKEY DIP

Serving: 8

Ingredients:

- 1 pound turkey breasts, skinless, boneless, cooked and shredded
- 10 ounces coconut cream

- 1 cup coconut milk
- A pinch of salt and black pepper
- ½ teaspoon garlic powder
- ¼ cup green onions, chopped

Directions:

- In your slow cooker, combine all the ingredients, cover and cook on low for 3 hours.
- Divide into bowls and serve.

Nutrition:

- Calories - 262
- Fat - 14,1
- Carbs - 24,1
- Protein - 10,9

SLOW COOKER CHEESE DIP

Serving: 8

Ingredients:

- 2-pound Velveeta cheese
- 7 oz ground beef
- 1 red onion, chopped
- 1 chili pepper
- ½ cup water
- 1 tablespoon taco seasoning
- 1 teaspoon salt
- 1 tablespoon olive oil
- 1 tablespoon dried dill

Directions:

- Put the olive oil in the skillet. Add the chopped onion, ground beef, salt, dried dill, and taco seasoning.
- Chop the chili pepper and add it to the meat mixture too.
- Close the lid and cook the meat mixture for 10 minutes or until is it totally cooked.
- Put the meat mixture in the slow cooker. Add water and Velveeta cheese.
- Stir gently. Close the slow cooker lid and cook the dish on HIGH for 2 hours.
- When the cheese is melted, stir it gently again.
- Serve it.

Nutrition:

- Calories - 363
- Fat - 21.3
- Carbs - 16.28
- Protein - 26

SPICED WALNUTS

Serving: 4

Ingredients:

- 1 pound walnut halves
- 2 tablespoons coconut oil, melted
- 1 tablespoon chili powder
- 1 teaspoon oregano, dried
- ¼ teaspoon garlic powder

- 1 teaspoon thyme, dried
- ½ teaspoon cayenne pepper

Directions:

- In your slow cooker, mix all the ingredients, cover and cook on low for 2 hours and 30 minutes.
- Divide into bowls and serve them warm.

Nutrition:

- Calories - 769
- Fat - 74,1
- Carbs - 12,9
- Protein - 27,6

SIMPLE MEATBALLS

Serving: 4

Ingredients:

- 1 and ½ pounds beef, ground
- 1 egg, whisked
- 16 ounces canned tomatoes, crushed
- 14 ounces canned tomato puree
- ¼ cup parsley, chopped
- 2 garlic cloves, minced
- 1 yellow onion, chopped
- Black pepper to the taste

Directions:

- In a bowl, mix beef with egg, parsley, garlic, black pepper and onion and stir well.
- Shape 16 meatballs, place them in your slow cooker, add tomato puree and crushed tomatoes on top, cover and cook on Low for 8 hours.
- Arrange them on a platter and serve.
- Enjoy!

Nutrition:

- Calories - 160
- Fat - 5
- Carbs - 10
- Protein - 7

BACON SKEWERS

Serving: 5

Ingredients:

- 1 cup ground pork
- ½ cup ground beef
- 4 oz bacon, sliced
- 1 tablespoon butter
- 1 teaspoon Italian seasoning
- 1 teaspoon salt
- 1 tablespoon crushed tomatoes
- ¼ cup heavy cream

Directions:

- In the mixing bowl, mix up together ground pork, ground beef, Italian seasoning, and salt.
- Then make the meatballs from the meat mixture.
- Wrap every meatball in the sliced bacon and string the meatballs on the skewers.
- Mix up together crushed tomatoes with cream and pour the liquid in the crockpot.
- Add the prepared meatball skewers and cook appetizer for 3 hours on High.

Nutrition:

- Calories - 380
- Fat - 28.9
- Carbs - 0.8
- Protein - 27.3

JALAPENO TAQUITOS

Serving: 5

Ingredients:

- 5 corn tortillas
- 4 oz Cheddar cheese, shredded
- 9 oz chicken fillets
- 3 oz cream cheese
- 1 tablespoon cilantro
- 1 cup water
- 1 teaspoon salt
- 1 teaspoon ground black pepper
- 2 jalapeno peppers

- 1 teaspoon onion powder

Directions:

- Place the chicken fillets in the slow cooker. Sprinkle the meat with the cream cheese, cilantro, salt, ground black pepper, and onion powder.
- Chop the jalapeno peppers and add them in the slow cooker bowl. Add water and close the slow cooker lid.
- Cook the dish for 8 hours on LOW.
- When the time is done, open the slow cooker lid and shred the chicken well.
- Place the shredded chicken mixture and shredded cheese in the tortillas and wrap.
- Place the dish in the preheated 350 F oven and cook for 10 minutes.
- Remove the dish from the oven and enjoy.

Nutrition:

- Calories - 285
- Fat - 14.9
- Carbs - 27.09
- Protein - 12

DESSERTS

COCONUT CAKE WITH CHOCOLATE TOPPING

Serving: 8

Ingredients:

- 1 cup coconut flour
- 2/3 cup almond meal
- 1 tsp baking powder
- 1 cup coconut oil
- 2 large eggs
- ¼ cup swerve
- 1 tsp vanilla extract
- ¼ cup cocoa powder, unsweetened
- 1 tsp stevia powder
- 1 cup whipped cream

Directions:

- In a large mixing bowl, combine coconut flour, almond meal, baking powder, and swerve. Crack eggs and beat well on medium speed. Now add 2/3 cup coconut oil and continue to mix until fully incorporated.
- Brush a 7-inches springform pan with some oil and dust with some cocoa powder. Plug in your instant pot and pour in 1 cup of water. Set the trivet at the bottom and put the wrapped springform on top. Seal the lid and set the steam release handle to the "SEALING" position.

- Set the timer for 25 minutes.
- When done, press the "CANCEL" button and perform a quick release by moving the
- pressure valve to the "VENTING" position.
- Open the lid and gently remove the pan. Cool to a room temperature.
- Meanwhile, press the "SAUTE" button on your instant pot. Add the remaining coconut oil, vanilla extract, stevia powder, and cocoa powder. Stir vigorously and add whipped cream. Cook for 1 minute. Press the "CANCEL" button again and remove the chocolate sauce from the instant pot.
- Drizzle the chilled cake with the chocolate sauce and refrigerate for 1 hour before serving.

Nutrition:

- Calories - 426
- Fat - 39.3g
- Carbs - 7.3g
- Protein - 6.6g

LIME CHEESECAKE

Serving: 2

Ingredients:

- 24 oz cream cheese
- 3 eggs
- 1 cup gluten-free sweetener
- ½ tbsp vanilla
- 1/4 cup lime juice

Directions:

- Mix all ingredients thoroughly using a mixer in a bowl.
- Pour 2 to 3 cups of water in the crockpot and place the bowl inside.
- Cover and cook for 2 hours and 30 minutes on high.

Nutrition:

- Calories - 219
- Fat - 16.7 g
- Carbs - 5.7 g
- Protein - 8 g
- Serving suggestions: Serve with any low-sugar fruit sauce or sliced fruits.

CARAMEL AND PEAR PUDDING

Serving: 7

Ingredients:

- ½ cup sugar
- ½ teaspoon ground cinnamon
- 1 ½ teaspoons baking powder
- 1/8 teaspoon ground cloves
- ¼ teaspoon salt
- 3/4 cup milk
- 4 medium pears, peeled and cubed
- ½ cup pecans, chopped
- ¾ cup brown sugar
- ¼ cup softened butter

Directions:

- Place all ingredients in the Instant Pot.
- Give a good stir to incorporate all ingredients.
- Close the lid and press the Manual button.
- Adjust the cooking time to 15 minutes
- Allow to chill in the fridge before serving.

Nutrition:

- Calories - 274
- Carbs - 47 g
- Protein - 3g
- Fat - 9g

SNACK CHICKPEAS

Serving: 9

Ingredients:

- 1-pound chickpea, canned, drained
- 4 oz white onion
- 1 tablespoon minced garlic
- 1 tablespoon chili flakes
- ½ teaspoon thyme
- ½ teaspoon ground coriander
- 1 teaspoon salt
- 12 oz chicken stock
- ½ cup fresh dill
- 1 teaspoon butter
- 3 tablespoon bread crumbs

Directions:

- Peel the white onion and grate it. Combine the grated onion with the minced garlic, chili flakes, thyme, ground cinnamon, salt, and butter.
- Put the canned chickpeas in the slow cooker.
- Add the chicken stock and grated onion mix. Close the slow cooker lid and cook the dish on HIGH for 4 hours. Meanwhile, wash the fresh dill and chop it.
- When the chickpeas are cooked, strain the excess liquid and place the chickpeas in a big bowl. Sprinkle with the bread crumbs and chopped fresh dill.
- Stir it carefully then serve the snack.

Nutrition:

- Calories - 270
- Fat - 5.3
- Carbs - 44.09
- Protein - 13

STEAMED LEMON CAKE

Serving: 8

Ingredients:

- ½ cup all-purpose flour
- 1 ½ cups almond flour
- 3 tablespoon white sugar
- 2 teaspoon baking powder
- ½ teaspoon xanthan gum

- ½ cup whipping cream
- ½ cup butter, melted
- 1 tablespoon juice, freshly squeezed
- Zest from one large lemon
- 2 eggs

Directions:

- Place a steamer in the Instant Pot and pour a cup of water.
- In a bowl, mix all the ingredients until well combined.
- Pour the batter into a dish that will fit inside the Instant Pot.
- Put aluminum foil on top.
- Place on the steamer and close the lid.
- Press the Manual button and adjust the cooking time for 30 minutes.
- Do natural pressure release.

Nutrition:

- Calories - 350
- Carbs - 11.1g
- Protein - 17.6 g
- Fat - 32.6g

VANILLA CAKE

Serving: 6-8

Ingredients:

- 1 cup water
- ½ cup unsalted butter, melted
- ¾ cup stevia sweetener
- 4 large eggs, beaten
- 1½ cups all-purpose flour
- ¾ cup heavy cream
- 2 tsp baking powder
- ½ tbsp vanilla extract
- ¼ tsp salt

Directions:

- Prepare the Instant Pot by adding the water to the pot and placing the steam rack in it.
- In a bowl, whisk together butter, stevia sweetener, and eggs until combined.
- Stir in the flour, heavy cream, baking powder, vanilla extract, and salt. Stir the mixture until just smooth.
- Grease a 7- to 8-inch baking pan with butter. Pour the batter in the pan and cover with foil.
- Place the pan on the rack. Close and lock the lid.
- Select the MANUAL setting and set the cooking time for 40 minutes at HIGH pressure.
- Once cooking is complete, let the pressure
- Release Naturally for 10 minutes. Release any remaining steam manually. Uncover the pot.
- Let the cake cool for a few minutes and serve.

ALMOND CAULIFLOWER SPREAD

Serving: 4

Ingredients:

- 3 cups cauliflower florets
- ½ cup almonds, soaked overnight and drained
- 2 cups almond milk
- 1 teaspoon garlic powder

Directions:

- In your slow cooker, combine all the ingredients, cover and cook on low for 7 hours.
- Blend using an immersion blender, divide into bowls and serve.

Nutrition:

- Calories - 191
- Fat - 5
- Carbs - 11
- Protein - 6

VANILLA CUPCAKES WITH CREAM FROSTING

Serving: 8

Ingredients:

- ½ cup butter, softened
- 3 eggs

- 1 ½ cup almond flour
- ½ cup swerve
- 2 tsp vanilla extract, divided in half
- 1 ½ tsp baking powder
- 1 cup cream cheese
- ¼ cup whipping cream
- 3 tbsp. powdered erythritol

Directions:

- In a large bowl, combine together almond flour and swerve. Add softened eggs, butter, and one teaspoon of vanilla extract. Using a hand mixer beat well on high speed until completely incorporated. Plug in your instant pot and set the trivet at the bottom of the stainless steel insert. Pour in one cup of water and gently place the muffin cups on top. Cover loosely with some aluminum foil and seal the lid.
- Set the steam release handle to the "SEALING" position and press the "MANUAL" button.
- Set the timer for 15 minutes.
- When done, perform a quick release by moving the pressure valve to the "VENTING" position and open the lid. Carefully remove the cups and Meanwhile, combine the remaining ingredients in a large mixing bowl. Beat well on high speed until light and fluffy. Top each cupcake with this mixture and refrigerate for 30 minutes before serving.

Nutrition:

- Calories - 262

- Fat - 25.8g
- Carbs - 9.4g
- Protein - 5.5g

CREAMY KETO COCONUT CAKE

Serving: 10

Ingredients:

- 2 cups coconut flour
- 3 teaspoon baking powder
- 1/4 cup granulated stevia
- 2 cups whipping cream; sugar-free
- 1 cup coconut cream
- 5 large eggs
- 3 tablespoon hazelnuts; finely chopped
- 1/4 cup almond flour
- 3 tablespoon shredded coconut
- 2 teaspoon vanilla extract

Directions:

- Plug in the instant pot and pour in one cup of water. Position a trivet at the bottom of the inner pot and set aside
- In a large mixing bowl, combine all dry ingredients and mix well. Add eggs, one at the time, and beat well on medium-high speed.
- Now add coconut cream and vanilla extract. Continue to beat for 2 more minutes on medium speed
- Grease a small springform pan with some coconut oil and pour in the mixture. Place in the

pot and seal the lid. Set the steam release handle and press the "MANUAL" button. Set the timer for 20 minutes on high pressure.
- Meanwhile, beat well the whipping cream until light and fluffy. Add chopped hazelnuts and optionally some finely chopped almonds.
- Refrigerate until use
- When you hear the cooker's end signal, perform a quick pressure release and open the lid. Remove the pan from the pot and cool for a while
- Top with whipped cream and refrigerate for 2-3 hours before serving

Nutrition:

- Calories - 217
- Fat - 18.2g
- Carbs - 5.1g
- Protein - 5.8g

CINNAMON APPLES

Serving: 6

Ingredients:

- 1 cup coconut sugar
- 6 apples, cored and halved
- 3 tablespoons ground cinnamon
- 2 teaspoons vanilla extract
- 1/2 cup apple juice
- 3 cups chopped walnuts

Directions:

- In your slow cooker, combine all the ingredients, cover and cook on low for 2 hours.
- Divide into bowls and serve warm.

Nutrition:

- Calories - 649
- Fat - 37,3
- Carbs - 75,6
- Protein - 15,8

COCOA BALLS

Serving: 8

Ingredients:

- 2 cups coconut flour
- 1 cup coconut sugar
- ¾ cup cocoa powder
- 1/2 teaspoon baking soda
- 2 tablespoons lemon juice
- 2 eggs, whisked
- 1 cup coconut milk
- ½ cup coconut oil, melted
- 2 teaspoons vanilla extract

Directions:

- In a bowl, combine all the ingredients except the coconut oil.
- Mix well.

- Add the coconut oil to your slow cooker then add the cookie mix. Spread the cookie mix in the pan, cover and cook on low for 4 hours. Take
- spoonful's
- of the mix and shape into balls and serve cold.

Nutrition:

- Calories - 333
- Fat - 23,5
- Carbs - 33,4
- Protein - 4,1

CHOPPED STRAWBERRY PIE

Serving: 8

Ingredients:

- 1 cup butter
- 1 cup flour
- ½ cup sugar
- 1 cup strawberry
- 4 tablespoons sugar, brown
- 1 teaspoon vanilla extract
- 2 tablespoons almond flour
- 1 teaspoon ground cinnamon

Directions:

- Cut the butter and combine it with the flour using your hands. Then add the almond flour and ground cinnamon. Mix it well to get a smooth, sticky dough.

- Wrap the dough in the plastic wrap and put it in the freezer for 10 minutes. Meanwhile, chop the strawberries and put them in the blender.
- Add the sugar and brown sugar. Then add the vanilla extract and blend the strawberries until they have the texture of jam. Remove the dough from the freezer and chop it into the tiny pieces. Then separate the chopped dough into 2 parts.
- Put the first part of the dough in the slow cooker.
- Then cover it with the strawberry blended mixture. After this, add the second part of the chopped dough and close the lid.
- Cook the pie for 7 hours on LOW. When the pie is cooked, chill and slice. Enjoy!

Nutrition:

- Calories - 310
- Fat - 23.4
- Carbs - 23.94
- Protein - 2

SHRIMP AND CABBAGE BOWLS

Serving: 4

Ingredients:

- 2 pounds shrimp, peeled and deveined
- 1 yellow onion, chopped
- 1 green cabbage, shredded
- ½ cup chicken stock

Directions:

- In your slow cooker, combine all the ingredients, cover and cook on low for 2 hours.
- Divide into bowls and serve.

Nutrition:

- Calories - 326
- Fat - 4,1
- Carbs - 16,5
- Protein - 54,3

EASY CHOCOLATE CAKE

Serving: 8

Ingredients:

- 1 cup skim milk
- 2 cups brown sugar
- 1 cup cocoa powder
- 1 teaspoon baking soda
- 1 tablespoon vinegar
- ¼ teaspoon salt
- 2 cups flour
- 3 eggs
- 1 tablespoon caster sugar

Directions:

- Beat the eggs in the mixer bowl and add the skim milk, salt, and baking soda.

- After this, add the vinegar and whisk. Then sift the flour into the egg mixture. Add the brown sugar and cocoa powder. Mix it carefully until you get a smooth dough.
- The texture of the dough should be like sour cream. Cover the slow cooker bowl with the parchment and pour the cocoa dough there.
- Close the lid and set the LOW regime.
- Cook the chocolate cake for 3.5 hours.
- Check if the cake is cooked by inserting a toothpick into the cake- if it comes out clean, it is done!
- Then remove it from the slow cooker or cook it for 30 minutes more (depending on the level of readiness of the cake. Chill the chocolate cake and sprinkle it with the caster sugar.
- Enjoy!

Nutrition:

- Calories - 419
- Fat - 5.4
- Carbs - 89.43
- Protein - 10

COCONUT CASHEWS

Serving: 6

Ingredients:

- 2 cups raw cashews, halved
- 1/3 cup coconut sugar
- 5 tablespoons coconut oil

- 1 cup coconut flakes, unsweetened

Directions:

- In your slow cooker, combine all the ingredients, cover and cook on high for 2 hours.
- Divide into cups and serve cold.

Nutrition:

- Calories - 449
- Fat - 37
- Carbs - 28,1
- Protein - 7,4

DELICIOUS QUICHE

Serving: 2

Ingredients:

- 3 large eggs
- ¼ cup milk
- Salt and ground black pepper to taste
- 1 tbsp chives, chopped
- ½ cup cheddar cheese, shredded
- Cooking spray
- 1 cup water

Directions:

- In a medium bowl, whisk together eggs, milk, salt, pepper, and chives until combined.
- Grease a 7- to 8-inch baking pan with cooking spray. Add the cheese to the pan.

- Pour the egg mixture into the pan and spread evenly.
- Pour the water into the Instant Pot and set a steam rack in the pot.
- Place the pan on the rack. Close and lock the lid.
- Select the MANUAL setting and set the cooking time for 30 minutes at HIGH
- pressure.
- Once timer goes off, use aQuick Release. Carefully unlock the lid.
- Serve.

KETO PECAN BROWNIES

Serving: 6

Ingredients:

- 4 tablespoon butter
- 1/4 cup pecans; finely chopped
- 1/2 cup almond flour
- 1/3 cup cocoa powder; unsweetened.
- 2 large eggs
- 1/3 cup swerve
- 4 tablespoon dark chocolate chips; sugar-free
- 2 tablespoon plain Greek yogurt
- 2 teaspoon baking powder
- 1/2 teaspoon cinnamon powder
- 1 teaspoon vanilla extract

Directions:

- Line a small cake pan with some parchment paper and lightly coat with some cooking spray. Set asde
- Plug in the instant pot and position a trivet at the bottom of the stainless steel insert. Pour in two cups of water and set aside.
- In a large mixing bowl, combine together butter, eggs, and swerve. With a paddle attachment on, beat well for 2-3 minutes on medium-high speed
- Gradually add almond flour and baking powder, beating constantly.
- Finally, add the remaining ingredients and beat until completely incorporated. Loosely cover the pan with some aluminum foil and place in the pot. Seal the lid and set the steam release handle to the "SEALING" position. Press the "MANUAL" button and set the timer for 15 minutes on high pressure
- When done; perform a quick pressure release and open the lid. Remove the pan from the pot and Repeat the process with the remaining dough

Nutrition:

- Calories - 202
- Fat - 19.5g
- Carbs - 2.8g
- Protein - 5.1g

CHOCOLATE BUNDT CAKE

Serving: 10

Ingredients:

- 1 cup almond flour
- ½ cup cocoa powder, unsweetened
- 3 tbsp. walnuts, unsweetened
- 4 large eggs
- 4 tbsp. coconut oil, melted
- ½ cup heavy cream
- 1 tsp baking powder
- 1 tsp powdered stevia

Directions:

- Combine all dry ingredients in large mixing bowl. Mix well and then add eggs, coconut oil, and heavy cream.
- Using a hand mixer, beat until well combined.
- Grease a 6-inches bundt pan with some cooking spray. Pour in the batter and set aside.
- Plug in your instant pot and pour in 2 cups of water in the stainless steel insert. Position a trivet and place the bundt pan on top. Securely close the lid and adjust the steam release handle.
- Press the "MANUAL" button and set the timer for 20 minutes.
- Cook on high pressure.
- When you hear the cooker's end signal, press "Cancel" button and release the pressure naturally.

- Open the pot and let it chill to a room temperature before serving.
- Enjoy!

Nutrition:

- Calories - 137
- Fat - 12.9g
- Carbs - 1.9g
- Protein - 4.6g

DULCE DE LECHE

Serving: 4

Ingredients:

- 1 can sweetened condensed milk

Directions:

- Place a steamer basket in the Instant Pot and add 8 cups of water.
- Pour the condensed milk into a 16-ounce canning jar.
- Place the jar with the condensed milk on the steamer rack.
- Place the jar with condensed milk on the steamer rack.
- Close the lid and press the Steam button.
- Adjust the cooking time to 30 minutes.
- Do natural pressure release.

Printed in Great Britain
by Amazon

78423405R00124